Go D

Go Down, Moses!

Daily Devotions
Inspired by
Old Negro Spirituals

Edited by
Leonidas A. Johnson

Judson Press
Valley Forge

Go Down, Moses!
Daily Devotions Inspired by Old Negro Spirituals
© 2000 by Leonidas A. Johnson
All rights reserved.

Cover art: "Reparation Now" bronze sculpture by Bill Page.

Library of Congress Cataloging-in-Publication Data
Go down, Moses! : daily devotions inspired by old Negro spirituals / edited by Leonidas A. Johnson.
     p.   cm.
   Includes bibliographical references and index.
   ISBN 0–8170–1372–5 (pbk. : alk. paper)
     1. Devotional calendars. 2. Afro-Americans—Prayer-books and devotions—English. I. Johnson, Leonidas A., 1959–
BV4810.G52 2000
242–dc21   00–060285
Printed in the U.S.A.

06 05 04 03 02 01 00

10 9 8 7 6 5 4 3 2 1

In loving memory

of the many brave souls
who dared to stand in the face of adversity
with confidence in God, who suffered, bled,
and died for truth, justice, and liberty;
who followed the example of
our Lord and Savior, Jesus Christ,
laid a foundation of hope,
and cleared a path of encouragement
for we who believe
in freedom!

L.A.J.

Therefore we also, since we are surrounded by so great a cloud of witnesses, let us lay aside every weight, and the sin which so easily ensnares us, and let us run with endurance the race that is set before us, looking unto Jesus, … who for the joy that was set before Him endured the cross, despising the shame, …. For consider him that endured such hostility from sinners against Himself, lest you become weary and discouraged in your souls. (Hebrews 12:1–3)

Contents

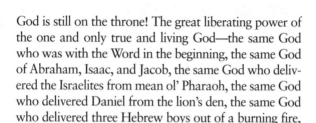
God is still on the throne! The great liberating power of the one and only true and living God—the same God who was with the Word in the beginning, the same God of Abraham, Isaac, and Jacob, the same God who delivered the Israelites from mean ol' Pharaoh, the same God who delivered Daniel from the lion's den, the same God who delivered three Hebrew boys out of a burning fire, the same God who sent his Son to set the captives free—is still available to us. God's liberating power can set anyone free (cf. John 8:31–32)!

Go Down, Moses!

The Holy Bible serves as a record of the liberating, wonder-working power of God. Throughout history, God's awesome power has stretched forth as a mighty, yet loving hand to the mistreated and misused, the weak and the worn, the forgotten and the forsaken, the downcast and the outcast, and the depressed and the oppressed. No where is God's power more evident than in its manifestation in the historical plight of African Americans.

Recorded in the African American slave songs and spirituals are precious jewels and treasures beyond compare. From the life experiences of these enslaved people comes a costly three-fold lesson about a God whose promises are true; a God who is too wise to make a mistake and too loving to be unkind; a God who sits high and looks low; a God who cares and is able to make a difference in our lives; a God who is able to change things, people, and circumstances; a God who can get us through our darkest midnight; a God who can make a way out of no way; a God who is able to deliver us from the fiery furnace of the harsh and miserable realities of living in a sin-filled world; a God who does have a plan for our lives; and a God who works in mysterious ways, his wonders to perform.

The important three-fold lesson we can learn from the experiences of our enslaved ancestors is:

1. We can't hurry God.
2. We can depend on God.
3. God is a strong Deliverer!

In other words, God may not come when we want, but God is always right on time. And when God shows up, God shows out! No, we can't hurry God, but we can depend on the Lord our God always. God is a strong Deliverer!

The application of this never-to-be-forgotten history lesson can be summarized in the words: "Trust in the Lord with all thine heart; and lean not unto thine own understanding. In all thy ways acknowledge him, and he shall direct thy paths" (Proverbs 3:5–6, KJV). Too many people suffered and died to learn this invaluable lesson. Let us never forget it!

The Scripture Readings

This devotional is organized to guide readers through the first five books of the Old Testament, also known as the Pentateuch (Torah, Law), plus Joshua, the first four books of the New Testament (the Gospels), plus Acts, and Revelation.

A major focus of the Pentateuch (Genesis, Exodus, Leviticus, Numbers, and Deuteronomy) is God's holiness. The Law required humankind to reestablish and maintain fellowship with the holy God who would save them from sin and death. According to God's plan of salvation, God raised up a people, known as the Israelites, through whom God would: (1) be revealed as the one and only, true and living God; and (2) bless all the peoples of the world. When God's people were enslaved by a ruler of Egypt, through a miraculous display of power and might, God destroyed the idol gods of Egypt, along with Pharaoh's mighty army, and delivered Israel out of bondage. The Book of Joshua is a continuation of the saga of God's chosen people and recounts their crossing the Jordan River to enter the Promised Land.

A major thrust of the Gospels is on the coming of the Messiah and the fulfillment of God's Law. There had been problems in the Promised Land after Israel inhabited the land. While in the Promised Land, the chosen people had failed repeatedly to keep God's commandments. For generations Israel continued on a cycle of disobedience, suffering, and repentance, followed by short-lived obedience. Because of humanity's inability to successfully deal with the problem of sin, God's only begotten Son took off his robe in glory, stepped down through forty-two generations and put on a human garment of love. Jesus suffered, bled, and died for the remission of our sins. By the grace of God, through faith in Jesus Christ, all people now can be justified before a holy God. Fellowship between God and humanity can be restored. Deliverance from the yoke of sin and eternal death is now possible. What wonder working power is found in the blood of Jesus! That's the good news!

Readings from the Book of Acts have been included because this book recounts the spread of the good news of the gospel message. May the accounts of the miraculous acts of the apostles, through the power of the Holy Spirit, serve to strengthen our faith in the power of the gospel message preached.

The Book of Revelation details the second coming of Jesus Christ. Jesus first came into the world as Savior and revealed himself as a meek and humble servant. At his second coming, Jesus will reveal himself as a champion Warrior and an instrument of God's wrath. Our victory over sin is not yet complete; for we are wrapped in mortal flesh and live in a sinful world. When he comes again, Christ will deliver the final blow to sin and death and claim ultimate victory over Satan, our enemy. Jesus will deliver the world from the works of the evil one and lead us into the heavenly and eternal Promised Land.

All of the Scripture readings featured in Go Down, Moses! were carefully selected to help readers strengthen their trust in God and faith in Jesus. Following the suggested daily reading guide will enable users to read these books in their entirety in one year.

Additionally, every other day includes a reading from either Proverbs or Psalms. The Book of Psalms centers around humanity's vertical relationship with God and emphasizes expressions from the inner most chambers of the human soul (cf. Matt. 22:37–38). The Book of Proverbs emphasizes the importance of horizontal (human-to-human) relationships and emphasizes practical knowledge and wisdom (cf. Matt. 22:39). Both Psalms and Proverbs offer practical wisdom to help believers grow in obedience to God (cf. Matt. 22:40). These readings also are arranged so that both books will be completed in one year.

Go Down, Moses! includes an optional Bible reading guide for persons who wish to read through the entire Bible in one year. The Bible-in-One-Year (BIOY) daily Scripture reading is located at the bottom of each page. For those reading through the entire Bible, a daily count is provided at the bottom of the page to indicate the number of days that have passed and how many days remain in the 365–day plan (current day/days remaining). For example, if you begin the BIOY guide on Day 1, after twenty weeks, you will see "(140/225)" on that day's devotional. This represents the 140th day since you began on Day 1, with 225 days remaining before reading through the entire Bible.

You may wonder whether reading through the entire Bible is necessary or beneficial. All Christians should strive to read the entire Bible. God's Word tells us "All scripture is given by inspiration of God, and is profitable …" (2 Tim. 3:16–17).

The Spirituals

The first printed references to the religious folksongs of black Americans as a distinctive genre began to appear early in the nineteenth century. However, no one has determined precisely when the term "spiritual" was first used in print to apply to the religious folksongs of black Americans (Southern 1997, 180). Though spirituals have been referred to variously as "jubilee," "minstrel," "religious," "slave," or "folksongs," the term traditionally has been used as an umbrella for many cries and expressions of the human spirit in bondage (Walker 1979, 43).

Spirituals were born out of the belly of oppression and grew up in the prison of human bondage. Black slaves in America utilized and perfected such African modes as mythic histories, slave tales and chants, animal stories, religious shouts and songs, clandestine protest rhymes, and uniquely interpreted songs and verses from their Afri-American setting (Lovell 1972, 117). The African American spiritual is a record of the traditions, beliefs, customs, and longings of an oppressed people such as no individual literature could possibly possess (Lovell 1972, 117). African American spirituals are the heart of all other American music and comprise the taproot of the musical expression of the black religious experience (Walker 1979, 43).

Just as time and pressure can turn dark carbon matter into precious jewels of enduring strength and clarity, the many years and pressures associated with the dark matter of slavery, racial prejudice, and political-social-economic injustice has produced the African American spiritual, clearly a magnificent jewel of great strength and beauty.

Music for the spiritual lyrics contained in *Go Down, Moses!* can be found in the references cited, except Lovell and Southern (few exceptions).

The Scripture-Spirituals Connection

There is a parallel between Israel's deliverance out of bondage in Egypt, as recorded in the Bible, and the deliverance of African Americans out of slavery in North America, as recorded in African American history (including the slave narratives). The evidence of God's delivering power, as recorded in Scripture and in African American history (and captured in the old Negro spirituals), are juxtaposed to encourage believers to trust and obey God so that you, as a believer, also may experience God's delivering power in your personal life through Christ. The readings in Psalms and Proverbs are further designed to deepen your worship experience with God and enhance your growth in spiritual wisdom.

To trust God and to obey is God's way to live victoriously through hard times. Press on!

Hymn of Invocation

"Guide Me, O Thou Great Jehovah"
(Tune—Old Meter Hymn—8s,7s,4s)

1 GUIDE me, O Thou great Jehovah,
    Pilgrim through this barren land;
 I am weak, but Thou art mighty,
    Hold me with Thy powerful hand:
 Bread of Heaven, Feed me till I want no more;
 Bread of Heaven, Feed me till I want no more.

2 Open now the crystal fountain,
    Whence the healing streams do flow;
 Let the fiery, cloudy pillar Lead me
    all my journey thro':
 Strong Deliverer, Be Thou still
    my Strength and Shield;
 Strong Deliverer, Be Thou still
    my Strength and Shield.

3 When I tread the verge of Jordan,
    Bid my anxious fears subside;
 Bear me thro' the swelling current,
    Land me safe on Canaan's side:
 Songs of praises I will ever give to Thee;
 Songs of praises I will ever give to Thee.

(William Williams)

Slave Song

1   SEE these poor souls from Africa
        Transported to America:
    We are stolen and sold to Georgia,
        will you go along with me?
    We are stolen and sold to Georgia,
        go sound the jubilee.

2   See wives and husbands sold apart,
    The children's screams!—it breaks my heart;
    There's a better day a-coming,
        will you go along with me?
    There's a better day a-coming,
        go sound the jubilee.

3   O gracious Lord! When shall it be
    That we poor souls shall all be free?
    Lord, break them Slavery powers—
        will you go with me?
    Lord, break them Slavery powers,
        go sound the jubilee.

4   Dear Lord! Dear Lord! When Slavery'll cease,
    Then we poor souls can have our peace;
    There's a better day a-coming,
        will you go along with me?
    There's a better day a-coming,
        go sound the jubilee.

(Southern 1997, 158)

The Negro's Complaint
(Tune–"Old Hundred"–L.M.)

1   GREAT God dost thou from heav'n above
     View all mankind with equal love?
     Why dost thou hide thy face from slaves,
     Confin'd by fate to serve the knaves?

2   When stole and bought from Africa,
     Transported to America,
     Like the brute beast in market sold,
     To stand the heat and feel the cold.

3   To stand the lash and feel the pain,
     Expos'd to stormy snow and rain.
     To work all day and half the night,
     And rise before the morning light! …

4   Although our skin be black as jet,
     Our hair be friz'd and noses flat,
     Shall we for that no freedom have,
     Until we find it in the grave.

5   Hath heav'n decreed that Negroes must,
     By wicked men be ever curs'd
     Nor e'er enjoy our lives like men,
     But ever drag the gauling chain.

6   When will Jehovah hear our cries,
     When will the sons of freedom rise,
     When will for us a Moses stand,
     And free us from a Pharaoh's land.

(Lovell 1972, 106)

Meditation (Spiritual)
"Go Down, Moses!"

1   WHEN Israel was in Egypt's land:
        Let my people go;
    Oppressed so hard they could not stand,
        Let my people go.

Refrain:

    Go down, Moses, 'Way down in Egypt land,
      Tell ole Pharaoh, Let my people go.

2   "Thus saith the Lord," bold Moses said,
        Let my people go;
    "If not, I'll smite your first-born dead,"
        Let my people go.

3   No more shall they in bondage toil, …
        Let them come out with Egypt's spoil, …

4   When Israel out of Egypt came, …
        And left the proud oppressive land, …

5   O, 'twas a dark and dismal night, …
        When Moses led the Israelites, …

6   'Twas good old Moses and Aaron, too, …
        'Twas they that led the armies through, …

7   The Lord told Moses what to do, …
        To lead the children of Israel through, …

8   O come along, Moses, you'll not get lost, …
        Stretch out your rod and come across, …

9   As Israel stood by the water side, …
        At the command of God it did divide, …

10 When they had reached the other shore, …
        They sang the song of triumph o'er, …

11 Pharaoh said he would go across, …
        But Pharaoh and his host were lost, ….

12 Oh, Moses, the cloud shall clear the way, …
        A fire by night, a shade by day, …

13 You'll not get lost in the wilderness, …
        With a lighted candle in your breast, …

14 Jordan shall stand up like a wall, …
        And the walls of Jericho shall fall, …

15 Your foes shall not before you stand, …
        And you'll possess fair Canaan's land, …

16 'Twas just about in harvest-time, …
        When Joshua led his host divine, …

17 O let us all from bondage flee, …
        And let us all in Christ be free, …

18 We need not always weep and moan, …
        And wear these slavery chains forlorn, …

(Songs of Zion, 1981, 112–113)

Meditation (Spiritual)
"Dese Bones Gwine to Rise Again"

1 LORD, he thought he'd make a man,
      Dese bones gwine to rise again;
Made him out of mud and a little bit of sand,
      Dese bones gwine to rise again.

Refrain:
*   I know it, 'deed I know it,*
      Dese bones gwine to rise again.

2 "Adam, Adam, where art thou?" ...
      "Here, Marse Lord, I'se comin' down." ...

3 Thought he'd make a woman too; ...
      Didn't know 'xactly what to do....

4 Took a rib from Adam's side; ...
      Made Miss Eve for to be his bride....

5 Put 'em in a garden rich an' fair; ...
      Tole 'em to eat what they found dere....

6 To one tall tree dey mus' not go; ...
      Dere mus' de fruit forever grow....

7 Ol' Miss Eve come a-walkin' roun'; ...
      Spied dat tree all loaded down....

8 Sarpent he came roun' de trunk, ...
      At Miss Eve his eye he wunk....

9 Firs' she took a little pull; ...
      Den she filled her apron full....

10 Adam he come prowlin' roun'; ...
      Spied dem peelin's on the groun' ...

11 Den he took a little slice; ...
      Smack his lips an' said 'twas nice ...

12   Lord, he spoke with a mighty voice, ...
      Shook de heavens to de joists....

13   "Adam! Adam! Where are thou?" ...
      "Yes, Marse Lord, I'se a-comin' now." ...

14   "You et my apples, I believe?" ...
      "Not me, Lord, but I 'spec 'twas Eve." ...

15   Lord den rose up in his wrath; ...
      Tole 'em beat it down de path....

16   "Out of my garden you mus' git, ...
      "For you an' me has got to quit." ...
      Dese bones gwine to rise again.

(Lovell, 1972, 256)

Go Down, Moses! *includes an optional Bible reading guide for persons who wish to read through the entire Bible in one year. The* **Bible-in-One-Year** *(BIOY) daily Scripture reading is located at the bottom of each page. For those reading through the entire Bible, a daily count is provided at the bottom of the page to indicate the number of days that have passed and how many days remain in the 365-day plan (current day/days remaining). For example, if you begin the BIOY guide on Day 1, after twenty weeks, you will see "(140/225)" on that day's devotional. This represents the 140th day since you began on Day 1, with 225 days remaining before reading through the entire Bible.*

Genesis 1-2
"A Little Talk wid Jesus Makes It Right"

1   O, A little talk wid Jesus, makes it right, all right;
    Little talk wid Jesus makes it right, all right.
    Lord, troubles of ev'ry kind,
    Thank God, I'll always find,
    Dat a little talk wid Jesus makes it right.

2   My brother, I remember when I was a sinner lost,
    I cried "Have mercy Jesus,"
        But still my soul was toss'd;
    'Til heard King Jesus say,
    "Come here, I am de way;"
    An' a little talk wid Jesus, makes it right.

3   Sometimes de forked lightnin',
        an' mutterin' thunder too,
    Of trials an' tem'-tation make it hard
        for me an' you,
    But Jesus, is our fr'en', He'll keep us to de en'
    An' a little talk wid Jesus makes it right.

(Johnson and Johnson 1926, 74)

Prayer Focus: Lord, thank you for listening to my cares and troubles and for being my Friend. Help me to be a good listener—both to you and to others.

BIOY: Genesis 1-3 (1/364)

Proverbs 1
"A Little Talk With Jesus"

1   BROTHER, pray, brother, pray,
   May the Lord help you pray,
   And a little talk with Jesus makes it right,
   All right, (All right,) All right, (All right,)
   And a little talk with Jesus makes it right.
2   Leader, pray, leader, pray, ...
3   Sister, pray, sister, pray, ...
4   Elder, pray, elder, pray, ...
5   Deacon, pray, deacon, pray, ...
6   Preacher, pray, preacher, pray, ...

                   (Boatner and Townsend 1927, 15)

Prayer Focus: Lord, thank you for listening to me again. Now I want to listen to you. Help me to be a better listener as we pray (talk) each day.

BIOY: Genesis 4-6 (2/363)

Genesis 3-4
"A New Hiding Place"

1   *OH, the rocks and the mountains shall all flee away,*
    And you shall have a new hiding place that day.
    Seeker, seeker, give up your heart to God,
    And you shall have a new hiding place that day.
2   Doubter, doubter, give up your heart to God, ...
3   Mourner, mourner, give up your heart to God, ...
4   Sinner, sinner, give up your heart to God, ...
5   Mother, mother, give up your heart to God, ...
6   Children, children, give up your heart to God, ...
                         (Boatner and Townsend 1927, 47)

Prayer Focus: Lord, thank you for protecting me from dangers seen and unseen. I don't want to run or hide from you ever again.

Proverbs 2
"Ain't Dat Good News?"

1   GOT a crown up in de Kingdom, (Leader)
ain't dat good news? (Response)
Got a crown up in de Kingdom,
ain't dat good news?

All: *I'm a-goin' to lay down dis world,*
Goin' to shoulder up mah cross,
Goin' to take it home to Jesus,
ain't dat good news?

2   Got a harp in de Kingdom, ...
3   Got a robe in de Kingdom, ...
4   Got a slippers in de Kingdom, ...
5   Got a Savior in de Kingdom, ...

(Songs of Zion 1981, 114)

Prayer Focus: Thank you, God, for the gift of eternal life through Christ Jesus. That's Good News!

BIOY: Genesis 10-13 (4/361)

4

Genesis 5-6
"Ain't You Glad?"

1   AIN'T you glad you got a hiding place?
    Ain't you glad you got a hiding place?
    Ain't you glad you got a hiding place,
        'Way over in the promised land?
2   My Lord gave me that hiding place, …
3   Ev'ry Christian's got a hiding place, …
4   There is no dying in that hiding place, …

(Boatner and Townsend 1927, 66)

Prayer Focus: It's going to rain, it's going to rain, and God's going to destroy the earth with fire next time. Lord, thank you for preparing an ark of safety for me. Sail me safely over the great white throne of judgment, far beyond the lake of fire and into the eternal promised land. Thank you for grace and mercy. Thank you for hiding me in the shadow of your love.

BIOY: Genesis 14-16 (5/360)

Proverbs 3
"All God's Chillun Got Wings"
(I've Got a Robe)

1   I GOT a robe, *you got a* robe,
All o' God's Chillun got a robe.
When I get to heab'n
I'm goin' to put on my robe,
I'm goin' to shout *all ovah God's Heab'n,*
Heab'n, Heab'n
Ev'rybody talkin' 'bout heab'n ain't goin' dere;
Heab'n, Heab'n,
I'm goin' to shout all ovah God's Heab'n.

2   I got-a wings, ... put on my wings, ... fly ...

3   I got a harp, ... take up my harp, ... play ...

4   I got shoes, ... put on my shoes, ... walk ...

(Johnson and Johnson 1925, 71)

Prayer Focus: Lord, I trust you. Thank you for directing my paths, for your correction, and for your promise of riches in glory in Christ Jesus.

BIOY: Genesis 17-19 (6/359)

Genesis 7-8
"All I Do, de Church Keep a-Grumblin'"

ALL I do, de church keep a grumblin',
All I do, Lord, all I do.
All I do, de church keep a grumblin',
All I do, I do, I do,
Yes, all I do, Lord, all I do.

1   Try my bes' for to serve my Master,
    Try my bes' for to serve my Lord;
    Try my bes' for to serve my Master,
    Hallelujah.

2   Try my bes' for to foller my Leader, ...

3   Kneel an' pray so de devil won't harm me, ...

4   I'm gwine cling to de ship o' Zion, ...

                            (Johnson and Johnson 1926, 130)

Prayer Focus: Lord, thank you for saving me. I love you and will do my best to trust and obey you always.

BIOY: Genesis 20-22 (7/358)

Proverbs 4
"All o' My Sins"

1   ALL o' my sins (All o' my sins) been taken away,
(taken away),
All o' my sins (All o' my sins) been taken away;
(taken away);
All o' my sins been taken away,
Glory, hallelujah to His name;
All o' my sins been taken away, taken away.

2   If I could (If I could) I surely would, …
Stand on the rock where Moses stood; …

3   My Lord done … just what He said, …
He healed the sick and He raised the dead; …

4   I went to valley … and I didn't go to stay, …
My soul got happy, I staid all day; …

(Boatner and Townsend 1927, 24)

Prayer Focus: Thank you, Lord, for wisdom and understanding. Open my eyes and ears to your truth.

BIOY: Genesis 23-26 (8/357)

Genesis 9–10
"Almost Over"

1 SOME seek de Lord and they don't seek him right
   Pray all day and sleep all night;
   And I'll thank God,
      almost over, almost over, almost over
   (My Lord) And I'll thank God, almost over.
2 Sister, if your heart is warm,
   Snow and ice will do you no harm.
3 I done been down, and I done been tried,
   I been through the water and I been baptized.
4 O sister, you must mind how you step on the cross,
   Your foot might slip, and your soul get lost.
5 An' when you get t' heavn' you'll be able for to tell,
   How you shunned the gates of hell.
6 Wrestle with Satan and wrestle with sin,
   Stepped over hell and come back agin.

                 (Allen, Ware, and Garrison 1867, 74)

Prayer Focus: Thank you, Lord, for you are my strength.

BIOY: Genesis 27–29 (9/356)

Proverbs 5
"Amen"

AMEN, Amen,
Amen, Amen, Amen.
Amen, (Oh Lawdy!)
Amen, (Have mercy!)
Amen, Amen, Amen.
(Sing it over now) Amen,
(Oh Lawdy) Amen,
(Have mercy) Amen, Amen, Amen.

(Songs of Zion 1981, 147)

Prayer Focus: Thank you for all the beautiful people in the world. Some of them even make me want to forget who I am. Lord, grant me wisdom and strength to resist the lust of my eyes and the lust of my flesh. Oh Lawdy!

BIOY: Genesis 30-33 (10/355)

DAY 11

Genesis 11-12
"Archangel Open the Door"

I AX all dem brudder* roun'
Brudder,* why can't you pray for me?
I ax all dem brudder* roun'
Brudder,* why can't you pray for me?

1 I'm gwine to my heaven,
   I'm gwine home,
   Archangel open de door;
   I'm gwine to my heaven,
   I'm gwine home;
   Archangel open de door.

2 Brudder, tuk off your knapsack, I'm gwine home;
   Archangel open de door.

(Allen, Ware, and Garrison 1867, 32)

* Sister

Prayer Focus: Jesus, you were unjustly crucified; my ancestors were unjustly lynched. How unfair death often comes! Thank God that death is a door to heaven.

BIOY: Genesis 34-36 (11/354)

Proverbs 6
"Balm in Gilead" (cf. Jer. 8:22)

THERE is a Balm in Gilead,
To make the wounded whole,
There is a Balm in Gilead,
To heal the sin-sick soul.

1 Sometimes I feel discouraged,
   And think my work's in vain,
   But then the Holy Spirit,
   Revives my soul again.

2 Don't ever feel discouraged,
   For Jesus is your friend,
   And if you lack for knowledge,
   He'll ne'er refuse to lend.

3 If you cannot preach like Peter,
   If you cannot pray like Paul,
   You can tell the love of Jesus,
   And say, "He died for all."

(Boatner and Townsend 1927, 43)

Prayer Focus: Jesus, sweet Savior, you are the Balm!

BIOY: Genesis 37-39 (12/353)

Genesis 13–14
"Before I'd Be a Slave (Oh, Freedom!)"

BEFORE I'd be a slave,
I'd be buried in my grave,
And go home to my Lord and be saved.

1 O, what preachin'! O, what preachin'!
   O, what preachin' *over me, over me!*
2 O, what mourning, …
3 O, what singing, …
4 O, what shouting, …
5 O, weeping Mary, …
6 Doubting Thomas, …
7 O, what sighing, …
8 O, Freedom, …

(Southern 1997, 217)

Prayer Focus: God, Jesus, and the Spirit make three; I will be free, with all that power in me!

BIOY: Genesis 40–42 (13/352)

Proverbs 7
"Bell da Ring"

I KNOW member, know Lord,
I know I yed-de de bell da ring.

1 Want to go to meeting, *Bell da ring,*
   Want to go to meeting, *Bell da ring.*
2 (Say) Road so stormy.
3 I can't get to meetin'.
4 De church mos' ober.
5 De heaven-bell a heaven-bell.
6 De heaven-bell I gwine home.
7 I shout for de heaven-bell.
8 Heaven 'nough for me one.
9 (Brudder) hain't you a member?

(Allen, Ware, and Garrison 1867, 34)

Prayer Focus: Lord, bless the gathering of believers.

BIOY: Genesis 43-45 (14/351)

Genesis 15-16
"Blow Your Trumpet, Gabriel"

1   DE talles' tree in Paradise,
    De Christian call de tree of life;
    And I hope dat trump might blow me home
    To de new Jerusalem.
    Blow your trumpet, Gabriel,
    Blow louder, louder;
    And I hope dat trump might blow me home
    To de new Jerusalem.
2   Paul and Silas, bound in jail,
    Sing God's praise both night and day;
    And I hope, &c

    (Allen, Ware, and Garrison 1867, 3)

Prayer Focus: Thank you for honoring your covenant with Abraham. I'm standing on your promises, walking in faith, and longing to come home and be with you forever.

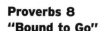

Proverbs 8
"Bound to Go"

1 I BUILD my house upon de rock, *O yes, Lord!*
   No wind, no storm can blow 'em down,
   O yes, Lord!
   March on, member, Bound to go;
   Been to de ferry, Bound to go;
   Left St. Helena, Bound to go;
   Brudder, fare you well.

2 I build my jouise on shiftin' sand,
   De first wind come he blow him down.

3 I am not like de foolish man,
   He build his house upon the sand.

4 One mornin' as I was a walkin' along,
   I saw de berries a-hanging down.

5 I pick de berries and I suck de juice,
   He sweeter dan de honey comb.

6 I tuk dem brudder, two by two,
   I tuk dem sister, tree by tree.

(Allen, Ware, and Garrison 1867, 22)

Prayer Focus: Jesus, you are the rock of my salvation.

BIOY: Genesis 49–50 (16/349)

Genesis 17-18
"Brother, Guide Me Home"

BRUDDER, guide me home an' I am glad,
Bright angels biddy me to come;
Brudder, guide me home an' I am glad,
Bright angels biddy me to come.

1　What a happy time, chil'n
　　What a happy time, chil'n,
　　What a happy time, chil'n,
　　Bright angels biddy me to come.

2　Let's go to God, chil'n,
　　Let's go to God, chil'n,
　　Let's go to God, chil'n,
　　Bright angels biddy me to come.

(Allen, Ware, and Garrison 1867, 86)

Prayer Focus: Lord, great is your faithfulness to the faithful. I covenant to trust you, love you, and love my neighbor. Nothing is too hard for you.

BIOY: Exodus 1-4 (17/348)

◎◎◎◎◎◎◎◎◎◎◎◎◎◎◎◎◎◎◎◎◎◎◎◎◎◎

Proverbs 9
"Brother Moses Gone"

BRUDDER Moses gone to de promised land,
Hal-le-lu, ha-le-lu-jah.

(Allen, Ware, and Garrison 1867, 49)

Prayer Focus: Jesus said, "And you shall know the truth, and the truth shall make you free" (John 8:32). As Jesus prayed to God he said, "Sanctify them by Your truth. Your word is truth" (John 17:17). The Bible reveals, "The fear of the Lord is the beginning of wisdom and the knowledge of the Holy One is understanding" (Prov. 9:10).

Lord, it is my prayer that you deliver me from the bondage of deception, lies, falsehoods, philosophical fallacies, practical blunders, and even from my own limited thinking. Lead me into the promised land of truth and understanding. Order my mental footsteps by your Word (cf. Ps. 119:105,133).

BIOY: Exodus 5-8 (18/347)

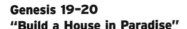

Genesis 19-20
"Build a House in Paradise"

1   MY brudder build a house in Paradise,
    My brudder build a house in Paradise,
    Build it wid-out a hammer or a nail,
    Build it wid-out a hammer or a nail.
2   My fader build a house in Paradise, …
3   O-na build a house in Paradise, …
                        (Allen, Ware, and Garrison 1867, 29)

Prayer Focus: Lord help me, day by day, to live in a meek and humble way. I want to live in a mansion not built with a hammer or a nail. Lord, guide me day by day in a pure and perfect way. I want to live in a house not made by hands. Lord, encourage me with a song, and don't forget to protect me from harm. Please give me grace to run this race to a building not made by hands. I'm just a traveler here sending up timber.

BIOY: Exodus 9-12 (19/346)

Proverbs 10
"Build Right on That Shore"

1 I'M going to *build* right on that shore,
  Lord, I'm going to *build* right on that shore,
  I'm going to *build* for my Jesus,
  Lord, for my Jesus ever more.
2 I'm going to *live* right on that shore, …
3 I'm going to *stand* right on that shore, …
4 I'm going to *wait* right on that shore, …
5 I'm going to *sing* right on that shore, …
6 I'm going to *shout* right on that shore, …
          (Boatner and Townsend 1927, 71)

Prayer Focus: Lord, I feel like a ship, tossed and driven on a restless sea of time. The storms of life are raging but I thank you that "I got my eye" on that bright celestial shore. I am bound for Canaan land; by and by I will make it to that happy golden strand, where my possessions lie.

BIOY: Exodus 13-15 (20/345)

Genesis 21-22
"By an' By"

O, BY an' by, by an' by
I'm gwinter lay down my heavy load.

1 I know my robes gwinter fit me well,
   I'm gwinter lay down my heavy load
   I tried it on at de gates of hell,
   I'm gwinter lay down my heavy load.

2 Hell is deep an' a dark despair,
   I'm gwinter lay down my heavy load
   O, stop po' sinner an' don't go dere,
   I'm gwinter lay down my heavy load.

(Johnson and Johnson 1925, 98)

Prayer Focus: I must tell Jesus all my problems. I cannot bear these burdens alone. Thank you, Lord, for your promise of blessing, for being my Provider, and for being a mighty good burden bearer!

BIOY: Exodus 16-18 (21/344)

Proverbs 11
"Calvary"

1 EV'RY time I think about Jesus,
   Ev'ry time I think about Jesus,
   Ev'ry time I think about Jesus,
   Sho'ly He died on Calvary.
2 Make me trouble — thinkin' 'bout dyin' …
   Calvary, Calvary,
   Calvary, Calvary,
   Calvary, Calvary,
   Sho'ly He died on Calvary.

(Johnson and Johnson 1925, 112)

Prayer Focus: On a hill called Calvary, the wicked nailed a battered and bruised Savior to a tree. Down south in a land called America, the wicked mercilessly beat enslaved Africans and hung them on trees. The wicked have not ceased from troubling. The weary long for rest. Lord, as Africans died to be free, let me live with victory. Satan, get behind! Victory is mine!

BIOY: Exodus 19–21 (22/343)

Genesis 23-24
"Can I Ride?"

IF I have my ticket, Lord, Can I ride?
If I have my ticket, Lord, Can I ride?
If I have my ticket, Lord, Can I ride?
Ride right up to heav'n right now?

1 Amazing grace! how sweet the sound,
   That saved a wretch like me;
   I once was lost, but now I'm found,
   Was blind, but now I see!

2 'Twas grace that taught my heart to fear,
   And grace my fears relieved;
   How precious did that grace appear,
   The hour I first believed!

3 Thro' many dangers, toils and snares,
   I have already come;
   'Tis grace hath bro't me safe thus far,
   And grace will lead me home.

4 The earth shall soon di-solve like snow,
   The sun forbear to shine;
   But God, who called me here below,
   Will be forever mine.

(Boatner and Townsend 1927, 76)

Prayer Focus: I love you, Lord! I got my ticket. I want to ride on to heaven when I die.

BIOY: Exodus 22-24 (23/342)

Proverbs 12
"Can't You Live Humble?"

CAN'T you live humble? Praise King Jesus!
Can't you live humble To de dyin' Lam'?

1 Lightnin' flashes, thunders roll,
   Make me think of my po' soul.
   Come here Jesus, come here, please,
   See me Jesus, on my knees.

2 Ev'rybody, come an' see,
   A man's been here from Galilee.
   Came down here, an' he talked to me,
   Went away an' lef' me free.

(Johnson and Johnson 1926, 138)

Prayer Focus: "Whoever loves instruction loves knowledge, But he who hates correction is stupid" (Prov. 12:1). Creator God, empower me by your indwelling Spirit to live humble and holy, meek and lowly. I want to be like Jesus.

BIOY: Exodus 25-28 (24/341)

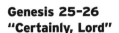

Genesis 25-26
"Certainly, Lord"

1 HAVE you got good religion? Cert'nly, Lord;
   Have you got good religion? Cert'nly, Lord;
   Have you got good religion? Cert'nly, Lord,
   Cert'nly, Cert'nly, Cert'nly, Lord.
2 Have you been redeemed? ...
3 Have you been to the pool? ...
4 Have you been baptized? ...
5 Is your name on high? ...
6 Has your name been changed? ...

(Boatner and Townsend 1927, 86)

Prayer Focus: There are some things I may not know;
but I am sure God is real and that the promises of God
are true. Great is God's faithfulness!

◎◎◎◎◎◎◎◎◎◎◎◎◎◎◎◎◎◎◎◎◎◎◎◎◎◎

Proverbs 13
"Changed Mah Name"

1   AH tol' Jesus it would be all right,
        if He changed mah name.
    Ah tol' Jesus it would be all right,
        if He changed mah name.
    Ah tol' Jesus it would be all right,
        if He changed mah name.
2   Jesus tol' me ah would have to live humble, …
3   Jesus tol' me that the world would be 'gainst me, …
4   But ah tol' Jesus it would be all right, …

                              (Songs of Zion 1981, 118)

Prayer Focus: Thank you, Lord, for changing me from
who I was to who I am. By your grace through faith, I
am a new creation in Christ Jesus (cf. 2 Cor. 5:17)! I
am, somebody! Hallelujah!

BIOY: Exodus 32-34 (26/339)

DAY 27

Genesis 27-28
"Children Do Linger"

1   O MEMBER, will you linger?
     See de chil'en do linger here.
2   I go to glory wid you,
     Member join.
3   O Jesus is our Captain ...
4   He lead us on to glory ...
5   We'll meet at Zion gateway ...
6   We'll talk dis story over ...
7   We'll enter into glory ...
8   When we done wid dis world trials ...
9   We done wid all our crosses ...
10   O brudder, will you meet us? ...
11   When de ship is out a-sailin' ...
12   O Jesus got de hellum ...
13   Fader, gader in your chil'en ...
14   O gader dem for Zion ...
15   'Twas a beauteous Sunday mornin'...
16   When he rose from de dead ...

(Allen, Ware, and Garrison 1867, 51)

Prayer Focus: Thank you, Lord, for the gate of heaven.

BIOY: Exodus 35-37 (27/338)

Proverbs 14
"Children Don't Get Weary"

CHILDREN, don't get weary,
Children, don't get weary,
Children, don't get weary,
We are newly born again.

1 Goin' to walk and talk together,
   Goin' to walk and talk together,
   Goin' to walk and talk together,
   We are newly born again.

2 Goin' to praise our Lord together, ...

3 Goin' to shake glad hands together, ...

4 Goin' to bend our knees together, ...

5 Goin' to sing glad songs together, ...

(Boatner and Townsend 1927, 80)

Prayer Focus: Thank you for your indwelling Spirit who empowers me to love my neighbor and to promote unity in diversity (cf. Rom. 8:11; Gal. 3:28).

BIOY: Exodus 38–40 (28/337)

Genesis 29-30
"Chilly Water"

CHILLY water, Chilly water,
Hallelujah to dat Lam';

1 I know dat water is chilly an' col',
   An' a *Hallelujah to dat Lam',*
   But I have Jesus in a my soul,
   An' a *Hallelujah to dat Lam';*

2 O' in a dat ark de little dove moaned, An' a ...
   Christ Jesus standin' as de corner stone, An' a ...

3 Ol' Satan' jes' like a snake in de grass, An' a ...
   He's watchin' for to bite you as a you pass, An'a ...

4 O, brothers and sisters one an' all, An' a ...
   You'd better be ready when de roll is call, An'a ...

(Johnson and Johnson 1926, 114)

Prayer Focus: Take me to the water to be baptized.
Lord, wash my mind and cleanse my heart.

DAY 30

Proverbs 15
"City Called Heaven"

1   I AM a poor pilgrim of sorrow,
    I'm tossed in this wide world alone,
    No hope have I for tomorrow,
    I've started to make heav'n my home.
    Sometimes I am tossed and driven,
    Lord, Sometimes I don't know where to roam,
    I've heard of a city called heaven,
    I've started to make it my home.

2   My mother has reached that pure glory,
    My father's still walkin' sin,
    My brothers and sisters won't own me,
    Because I am tryin' to get in.

(Songs of Zion 1981, 135)

Prayer Focus: Lord, I'm walking up the King's Highway. Help me make it to that city called heaven.

BIOY: Leviticus 4-7 (30/335)

Genesis 31–32
"Climbin' Up d' Mountain"

CLIMBIN' up d' mountain, children
(Good Lawd, Ah)
Didn't come here for to stay,
(Oh, my Lawd, and)
If ah nevermore see you again,
gonna meet you at de judgment day.
(Hallelujah, Lawd, Ah'm)

1   Hebrew children in de fiery furnace. *Oh Lawd,*
    And dey begin to pray, *Oh Lawd,*
    And de good Lawd smote dat fire out.
    Oh, wasn't dat a mighty day!
    Good Lawd, wasn't dat a mighty day!
2   Daniel went in de lions' den, *Oh Lawd,*
    And he begin to pray, *Oh Lawd,*
    And de angel of de Lawd locked de lions's jaw.
    Oh, wasn't dat a mighty day!
    Good Lawd, wasn't dat a mighty day!
                        (Songs of Zion 1981, 120)

Prayer Focus: Lord, give me strength to climb up the mountains of life.

BIOY: Leviticus 8–10 (31/334)

Proverbs 16
"Come Along, Moses"

COME along, Moses,
don't get lost, don't get lost, don't get lost,
Come along, Moses,
don't get lost, We are the people of God.

1 We have a just God to plead-a our cause,
   to plead-a our cause, to plead-a our cause,
   We have a just God to plead-a our cause,
   We are the people of God.

2 He sits in the Heaven and he answers prayer,
   he answers prayer, he answers prayer, …

3 Stretch out your rod and come across,
   and come across, and come across, …

(Allen, Ware, and Garrison 1867, 104)

Prayer Focus: I praise you, Lord. You are just and full of compassion. You are slow to anger, and great in mercy (Ps. 145:8). Thank you for answering prayer.

BIOY: Leviticus 11-14 (32/333)

Genesis 33-34
"Come Go with Me"

1 OLE Satan is a busy ole man,
   He roll stones in my way;
   Mass' Jesus is my bosom friend,
   He roll 'em out o' my way.
   O come-e go wid me,
   O come-e go wid me,
   O come-e go wid me,
   A walkin' in de heaven I roam.

2 I did not come here myself, my Lord,
   It was my Lord who brought me here;
   And I really do believe I'm a child of God,
   A-walkin' in de heaven I roam.

(Allen, Ware, and Garrison 1867, 57)

Prayer Focus: Lord, thank you for ordering my steps and for delivering me from the evil one.

BIOY: Leviticus 15-17 (33/332)

DAY 34

Proverbs 17
"Come Here, Lord"

COME here, Lord!
Come here, Lord!
Come here, Lord!
Sinner cryin' come here Lord.

1   O little did I think He was so nigh,
    Sinner cryin' come here, Lord.
    He spoke an' He made me laugh an' cry,
    Sinner cryin' come here, Lord.

2   O mourners if you will believe, ...
    De grace of God you will receive, ...

3   O seek God's face but don't seek right, ...
    Dey pray a lit'le by day an' none by night, ...

4   O sinner you had better pray, ...
    Satan's 'round you ev'ry day, ...

                              (Johnson and Johnson 1926, 176)

Prayer Focus: Lord, have mercy! Help me, Jesus.

BIOY: Leviticus 18–20 (34/331)

Genesis 35-36
"Come Out de Wilderness"
(How Did You Feel?)

1 TELL me, how did you feel when you
   come out the wilderness,
   come out the wilderness,
   come out the wilderness?
   How did you feel when you,
   come out the wilderness?
   Leaning on the Lord.
   I'm a-leaning on the Lord,
   I'm a-leaning on the Lord,
   I'm a-leaning on the Lord,
   Who died on Calvary.
2 Well, I loved ev'rybody when I, …
3 Well, my soul was happy when I, …

(Boatner and Townsend 1927, 13)

Prayer Focus: Revive me with joy and strength.

BIOY: Leviticus 21-24 (35/330)

Proverbs 18
"Come to Jesus"

1 COME to Jesus, Come to Jesus,
   Come to Jesus *just now;*
   Just now come to Jesus,
   Come to Jesus *just now.*
2 He will save you, …
3 He is willing, …
4 He is able, …
5 Come, confess him, …
6 Come obey him, …
7 He will hear you, …
8 He'll forgive you, …
9 He will cleanse you, …
10 Jesus loves you, …
11 Only trust him, …
   (The AME Zion Bicentennial Hymnal 1996, 408)

Prayer Focus: Lord, I come. Meet and greet me.

BIOY: Leviticus 25-27 (36/329)

Genesis 37-38
"Crucifixion"

1   THEY crucified my Lord,
    an' He never said a mumbalin' word;
    They crucified my Lord,
    an' He never said a mumbalin' word.
    Not a word, not a word, not a word.
2   They nailed him to the tree, ...
3   They pierced him in the side, ...
4   The blood came twinklin' down, ...
5   He bow'd His head an' died, ...

(Johnson and Johnson 1925, 174)

Prayer Focus: Remind me of the cross when life seems unfair. You did not have to leave your home in glory to be crucified but you did. They beat you, spat on you, and nailed you to an old rugged cross. You suffered, bled, and died for the remission of my sins. I'm so grateful. Thank you, Lord. I won't complain.

BIOY: Numbers 1-4 (37/328)

Proverbs 19
"Daniel Saw de Stone"
(cf. Dan. 2:34)

DANIEL saw de stone, Rollin', rollin',
Daniel saw de stone,
Cut out de mountain wid-out hands.

1   Nevah saw such a man befo'
     Cut out de mountain wid-out hands.
     Preachin' gospels to de po',
     Cut out de mountain wid-out hands.

2   Daniel pray'd in de lion's den...
     Spite o' all dem wicked men, ...

3   Pray'd an' pray'd three times a day...
     Drive de devil far away, ...

(Johnson and Johnson 1926, 162)

Prayer Focus: Lord, help me to pray daily and through the power of prayer, freely and boldly walk by faith though I may be enslaved, oppressed, and/or persecuted like many African American saints were.

BIOY: Numbers 5-7 (38/327)

Genesis 39-40
"De Angel Roll de Stone Away"

DE angel roll de stone away;
De angel roll de stone away;
'Twas on a bright an' shiny morn,
When de trumpet begin to soun';
De angel roll de stone away.

1 Sister Mary came a-runnin', at the break o' day,
Brought de news f'om heaben,
  De stone done roll away.

2 I'm a-lookin' for my Saviour, tell me where He lay,
High up on de mountain,
  De stone done roll away.

3 De soljahs dere a plenty, standin' by de do',
But dey could not hinder, De stone done roll away.

4 Ol' Pilate an' his wise men, didn't know what to say,
De miracle was on dem, De stone done roll away.

(Johnson and Johnson 1926, 118)

Prayer Focus: Lord, send an angel to roll away stones
of bigotry, prejudice, racial hatred, cultural intolerance,
and insensitivity that block my path.

BIOY: Numbers 8-10 (39/326)

Proverbs 20
"De Angels in Heab'n Gwinter Write My Name"

O, WRITE my name,
O, write my name;
O, write my name,
De Angels in de heab'n gwinter write my name.

1   Write my name when a you get home,
     De Angels in de heab'n gwinter write my name.
     Yes, write my name wid a golden pen,
     De Angels in de heab'n gwinter write my name.

2   Write my name in the Book of life,
     De Angels in de heab'n gwinter write my name.
     Yes, write my name in de drippin' blood,
     De Angels in de heab'n gwinter write my name.

(Johnson and Johnson 1926, 128)

Prayer Focus: Lord, I thank you for the promise of a better day and brighter tomorrow. I remain hopeful.

BIOY: Numbers 11-13 (40/325)

DAY 41

Genesis 41-42
"De Band o' Gideon" (cf. Judges 7:2)

1 OH, de band o' Gideon, band o' Gideon,
      band o' Gideon *over in Jordan,*
   Band o' Gideon, band o' Gideon
   how I long to see dat day.
2 Oh, de milk white horses, …
a *I hail to my sister, my sister she bow low,*
   Say, don't you want to go to heav'n
   How I long to see dat day.
b *I hail to dat mourner, dat mourner he bow low,*
   Say don't you want to go to heav'n
   How I long to see dat day.
3 Oh, de twelve white horses, …
4 Gwine to hitch 'em to de chariot, …

(Johnson and Johnson 1925, 156)

Prayer Focus: With you I can , I will, make it!

BIOY: Numbers 14-16 (41/324)

Proverbs 21
"De Blin' Man Stood on de Road an' Cried"

1 O, DE blin' man stood on de road an' cried,
   O, de blin' man stood on de road an' cried,
   Cryin' O, my Lord save-a me,
   De blin' man stood on the road an' cried,
   Cryin' what kind o' shoes am dose you wear,
   Cryin' what kind o' shoes am dose you wear,
   Cryin' O, my Lord save-a me,
   De blin' man stood on the road an' cried.

2 Cryin' dat he might receib his sight,
   Cryin' dat he might receib his sight,
   Cryin' O, my Lord save-a me,
   De blin' man stood on the road an' cried,
   Crying dese shoes I wear am de Gospel shoes,
   Crying dese shoes I wear am de Gospel shoes,
   Cryin' O, my Lord save-a me,
   De blin' man stood on the road an' cried.

(Johnson and Johnson 1925, 108)

Prayer Focus: Lord, my ears are not shut to the cry of the poor. Help me that I may help them.

DAY 43

Genesis 43-44
"De Gospel Train"

GIT on board, little children,
Git on board, little children,
Git on board, little children,
Dere's room for many a mo'.

1   De Gospel train's a comin',
    I hear it jus' at han',
    I hear de car wheels rumblin',
    An' rollin' thro' de lan'.

2   I hear de train a comin',
    She's comin' roun' de curve,
    She's loosened all her steam an' brakes,
    An' strain in' eb'ry nerve.

3   De fare is cheap an' all can go,
    De rich an' poor are dere,
    No second class aboard dis train,
    No diff'rence in de fare.

(Songs of Zion 1981, 116)

Prayer Focus: I want to board the gospel train. Thank you for letting me ride!

BIOY: Numbers 20-22 (43/322)

Proverbs 22
"De Ol' Ark's a-Moverin' an'
I'm Goin' Home"

O, DE ol' ark's a moverin', a moverin', a
moverin',
De ol' ark's a moverin', an' I goin' home.

1 See dat sister all dressed so fine?
  She ain't got Jesus on a her min'.

2 See dat brother all dressed so gay?
  O, death's gwinter come for to carry him away.

3 See dat sister dere comin' so slow?
  She wants to go to heab'n
      fore de heab'n door close.

4 'Tain't but one a thing on a my min',
  My sister's gone to heabin an' a lef' a me behin'.
  O, de ol' ark she reel, De ol' ark she rock,
  D' ol' ark she landed on de mountain top.
  O, de ol' ark's a moverin', a moverin', a moverin',
  De ol' ark's a moverin', an' I goin' home.

                    (Johnson and Johnson 1926, 25)

Prayer Focus: Keep me in the ark of safety.

BIOY: Numbers 23-26 (44/321)

Genesis 45-46
"De Ol' Sheep Done Know de Road"

OH, de ol' sheep done know de road,
De ol' sheep done know de road,
De ol' sheep done know de road,
De young lam's mus' fin' de way.

1   Oh, soon-a in de mornin' when I rise,
    De young lam's mus' fin' de way.
    Wid crosses an' trials on ev'ry side,
    De young lam's mus' fin' de way.

2   My brother ain't you got yo' accounts all sealed, ...
    You'd better go git 'em 'fore you leave dis fiel'....

3   Oh, shout a my sister for you are free, ...
    For Christ has bought yo' liberty....

4   I really do believe wid out a doubt, ...
    Dat de Christian has a right to shout....

(Johnson and Johnson 1926, 160)

Prayer Focus: You are my Shepherd. Lead me, guide me, along the way.

BIOY: Numbers 27-29 (45/320)

DAY 46

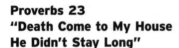

Proverbs 23
"Death Come to My House
He Didn't Stay Long"

HA-LE-LU-U, Hal-le-lu,
O, my Lord,
I'm gwinter see my mother again,
Hal-le-lu.

1   Death come to my house, he didn't stay long,
    I look on de bed, an' my *mother* was gone,
    I'm gwinter see my *mother* again, Ha-le-lu.

2   Death come to my house, he didn't stay long,
    I look on de bed, an' my *father* was gone,
    I'm gwinter see my *father* again, Hal-le-lu.

3   ... *sister* ...

4   ... *brother* ...

(Johnson and Johnson 1926, 108)

Prayer Focus: Thank you for the memories of loved ones death has taken away and for the opportunity to see them again in heaven's Canaan land.

BIOY: Numbers 30-32 (46/319)

Genesis 47-48
"Death's Gwinter Lay His
Cold Icy Hands on Me"
(Familiar Version)

DEATH is gwinter lay his icy cold hands on me.
Lord, on me
Death is gwinter lay his icy cold hands on me.

1   One mornin' I was walkin' 'long,
    I heard a voice an' saw no man;
    Said go in peace an' sin no mo',
    Yo' sins fo'giv'n an' yo' soul set free.

2   One o' dese mornin's it won't be long,
    You'll look fo' me, an' I'll be gone;
    Yes, one o' dese mornin's 'bout twelve o' clock,
    Dis ol' worl' am gwinter reel an' rock.

(Johnson and Johnson 1926, 93)

Prayer Focus: When it's time for me to go, lead me on home, Lord.

Proverbs 24
"Death's Gwinter Lay
His Cold Icy Hands on Me"
(Rare Version)

1 O SINNER, sinner, you better pray,
   Death's gwinter lay his cold icy hands on me,
   Or yo' soul will get los' at de judgment day,
   Death's gwinter lay his cold icy hands on me.

2 Some o' dese mornin's bright an' fair, ...
   I'll take my wings an' cleave de air, ...
   Cryin' O, Lord! Cryin' O, my Lord,
       Cryin' O, Lord!
   Death's gwinter lay his cold icy hands on me.

3 Yes, I'm so glad I've been redeem'd, ...
   I'm ready fo' to cross ol' Jordan's stream, ...

(Johnson and Johnson 1926, 96)

Prayer Focus: Death is swallowed up in victory. Thanks be to almighty God through Jesus (1 Cor. 15:55–57)!

BIOY: Deuteronomy 1-3 (48/317)

Genesis 49-50
"Deep Down in My Heart"

I'VE got good religion down in my heart;
In my heart, in my heart;
I've got good religion down in my heart;
Deep down in my heart.

1   *And I know I've been converted*
       down in my heart; In my heart, In my heart;
    Yes, I know I've been converted
       down in my heart;
    Deep down in my heart.

2   I can feel the Spirit moving …
3   There's a little wheel a-turning …
4   I can feel the fire burning …
5   There is joy, joy, joy …

(Boatner and Townsend 1927, 45)

Prayer Focus: Touch me, Lord Jesus, with thy hand of mercy. Cleanse me and make my heart thy throne!

BIOY: Deuteronomy 4-7 (49/316)

Proverbs 25
"Deep River"

DEEP river, my home is over Jordan;
Deep river, Lord, I want to cross over
*   into camp ground.*

1   Oh, don't you want to go to that gospel feast,
    That promised land, where all is peace?

2   I'll go into heav'n and take my seat,
    Cast my crown at Jesus' feet.

3   Oh, when I get to heav'n I'll walk all about,
    There's nobody there to turn me out.

(Boatner and Townsend 1927, 52)

Prayer Focus: Lord, I want to go to that distant land; take my hand and lead me home. Jesus, I know that you are waiting in that distant land; take my hand and show me the way.

BIOY: Deuteronomy 8–11 (50/315)

Exodus 1-2
"Dere's a Han' Writin' on de Wall"
(cf. Dan. 5:5)

DERE'S a han' writin' on de wall,
Dere's a han' writin' on de wall,
Oh, won't you come an' read it,
See what it say,
Dere's a han' writin' on de wall.

1   Oh, Daniel,
    Dere's a han' writin' on de wall.
    Who write de let'er?
    Dere's a han' writin' on de wall.

2   God write de let'er,
    Dere's a han' writin' on de wall.
    Tell Ol' Nebucaneezah dat
    he's weighed in de balance an' foun' wantin'.

(Johnson and Johnson 1926, 171)

Prayer Focus: Although I'm oppressed and in a foreign land, my peace rests in the knowledge that vengeance is yours (Rom. 12:19–21).

BIOY: Deuteronomy 12-13 (51/314)

Proverbs 26
"Dere's No Hidin' Place Down Dere"

DERE'S no hidin' place down dere,
Dere's no hidin' place down dere,
Oh I went to de rock to hide my face,
De rock cried out, "No hidin' place,"
dere's no hidin' place down dere.

1   Oh de rock cried, "I'm burnin' too,"
   Oh de rock cried, "I'm burnin' too,"
   Oh de rock cried out I'm burnin' too,
   I want a go to hebben as well as you,
   dere's no hidin' place down dere.

2   Oh de sinner man he gambled an' fell,
   Oh de sinner man he gambled an' fell,
   Oh de sinner man gambled, he gambled an' fell;
   he wanted to go to hebben, but he had to go to hell,
   dere's no hidin' place down dere.

(Johnson and Johnson 1925, 74)

Prayer Focus: I believe there is a heaven and a hell. Thank you for the assurance of salvation through Jesus Christ.

BIOY: Deuteronomy 14–15 (52/313)

Exodus 3–4
"Didn't My Lord Deliver Daniel?"

DIDN'T my Lord deliver Daniel,
*   deliver, Daniel, deliver Daniel,*
Didn't my Lord deliver Daniel,
*   An' why not every man.*

1 He delivered Daniel f'om de lions den,
    Jonah f'om de whale,
    An' de Hebrew chillun f'om de fiery furnace,
    An' why not every man.

A *De moon run down in a purple stream,*
    De sun forbear to shine,
    An' every star disappear, King Jesus shall-a be mine.

B *De win' blows eas' an' de win' blows wes',*
    It blows like de judgment day,
    An' ev'ry po' soul dat never did pray'll,
      be glad to pray dat day.

2 I set my foot on de Gospel ship,
    am' de ship begin to sail,
    It landed me over on Canaan's shore,
    An' I'll never come back no mo'.

(Johnson and Johnson 1925, 148)

Prayer Focus: Lord, you are my strong Deliverer!

BIOY: Deuteronomy 16–19 (53/312)

Proverbs 27
"Didn't Old Pharaoh Get Los'?"

DIDN'T old Pharaoh get los', get los'.
Didn't old Pharaoh get los'.
In de Red Sea.

1   Isaac a ransom,
        While he lay upon an altar bound;
    Moses an infant cast away,
        By Pharaoh's daughter found.
2   Joseph by his false brethren sold,
        God raised above them all;
    To Hannah's child the Lord foretold,
        How Eli's house should fall.
3   De Lord said unto Moses,
        "Go unto Pharaoh now,
    For I have hardened Pharaoh's heart,
        To me he will not bow."

(Johnson and Johnson 1925, 60)

Prayer Focus: Thank you for delivering me from the pharaohs I face. Before you only will I humbly bow.

Exodus 5✛-6
"Didn't Old Pharaoh Get Los'?" (cont.)

4   DEN Moses an' Aaron,
         To Pharaoh did go,
     "Thus says de God of Israel,
         Let my people go."

5   Old Pharaoh said,
         "Who is de Lord dat I should him obey?"
     "His name it is Jehovah,
         For he hears his people pray."

6   Hark! hear de children murmur,
         Dey cry aloud for bread,
     Down come de hidden manna,
         De hungry soldiers fed.

7   Den Moses numbered Israel,
         Through all de land abroad,
     Sayin', "Children, do not murmur,
         But hear de word of God."

(Johnson and Johnson 1925, 60)

Prayer Focus: I will not murmur; I will listen for your Word. I praise you!

BIOY: Deuteronomy 23-26 (55/310)

Proverbs 28
"Didn't Old Pharaoh Get Los'?" (cont.)

8   DEN Moses said to Israel,
        As dey stood along de Shore,
    "Yo' enemies you see today,
        You'll never see no more."
9   Den down come raging Pharaoh,
        Dat you may plainly see,
    Old Pharaoh an' his host
        Got los' in de Red Sea.
10   Den men an' women an' children,
        To Moses dey did flock;
    Dey cried aloud for water,
        An' Moses smote de rock.
11   An' de Lord spoke to Moses,
        From Sinai's smoking top,
    Sayin' "Moses lead de people,
        Till I shall bid you stop."

(Johnson and Johnson 1925, 60)

Prayer Focus: I praise you, Lord, for your mighty acts.

BIOY: Deuteronomy 27-30 (56/309)

Exodus 7-8
"Die in de Fiel'"

OH, what a you say, seekers,
    Oh, what a you say, seekers,
Oh, what a you say, seekers,
    About dat Gospel war.
An' what a you say, brothers,
    An' what a you say, brothers,
An' what a you say, brothers,
    About dat Gospel war.
An' I will die in de fiel', will die in de fiel',
will die in de fiel' I'm on my journey home.
(Sing it ovah)

(Johnson and Johnson 1925, 68)

Prayer Focus: Lord, open my eyes to spiritual warfare. I will not surrender. Victory shall be mine!

BIOY: Deuteronomy 31-32 (57/308)

〰️〰️〰️〰️〰️〰️〰️〰️〰️〰️〰️〰️〰️〰️〰️〰️

Proverbs 29
"Do Don't Touch-a My Garment, Good Lord, I'm Gwine Home"

1 DO don't touch-a my garment,
       Good Lord, Good Lord.
   Do don't touch-a my garment,
       Lord I'm gwine home.
2 To yo' God an' my God, …
3 Do don't touch-a my slippers, …
4 Oh, touch me not little Mary, …
5 Do don't touch-a my starry crown, …
6 Good Lord, Good Lord, …

(Johnson and Johnson 1926, 68)

Prayer Focus: Where there is no vision people perish. I thank you for the assurance of a better day and a brighter tomorrow in a heavenly home. You give my life meaning and purpose.

BIOY: Deuteronomy 33-34 (58/307)

DAY 59

Exodus 9-10
"Do, Lord, Remember Me"

DO, Lord, do, Lord, do, Lord, remember me!
Do, Lord, do, Lord, do, Lord, remember me!
Do, Lord, do, Lord, do, Lord, remember me!
'Way beyond the sun.

1   I've got a home in Beu-lah land,
    Outshines the sun; outshines the sun;
    I've got a home in the Beu-lah land,
    Outshines the sun,
    'Way beyond the sun.

2   I've got a robe in Beu-lah land, ...
3   I've got a crown in Beu-lah land, ...
4   I've got a mother in Beu-lah land, ...
5   I've got a Savior in Beu-lah land, ...

(Boatner and Townsend 1927, 54)

Prayer Focus: Lord, Your name is worthy to be praised in all the world. Do Lord, remember me.

Proverbs 30
"Don't Be Weary, Traveller"

DON'T be weary, traveller,
*   Come along home to Jesus;*
Don't be weary traveller, Come along to Jesus.

1   My head got wet with the midnight dew,
    Come along home to Jesus;
    Angels bear me witness too,
    Come along home to Jesus.

2   Where to go I did not know, ...
    Ever since he freed my soul, ...

3   I look at de worl' and de worl' look new, ...
    I look at de worl' and de worl' look new, ...

(Allen, Ware, and Garrison 1867, 75)

Prayer Focus: Lord, sometimes I feel so tired, don't know just what to do. Revive my soul and my spirit. Please make me feel brand new!

BIOY: Joshua 5-8 (60/305)

Exodus 11-12
"Don't Let it Be Said, Too Late"

1   MY mother she's gone, she's gone, she's gone,
   To enter the golden gate;
   My mother she's gone, she's gone, she's gone,
   To enter the golden gate.
   Don't let it be said, too late, too late,
   To enter the golden gate;
   Don't let it be said, too late,
   To enter the golden gate.

2   My father he's gone, he's gone, he's gone, ...

3   My sister she's gone, she's gone, she's gone, ...

4   My brother he's gone, he's gone, he's gone, ...

5   My Jesus He's gone, He's gone, He's gone, ...

(Boatner and Townsend 1927, 46)

Prayer Focus: Dear Lord Jesus, precious Lamb of God, I repent of all my sins. I surrender all to you.

BIOY: Joshua 9-12 (61/304)

Psalm 1
"Don't Stay Away"

1   BROTHERS, don't stay away,
> Brothers, don't stay away,
Brothers, don't stay away, don't stay away,
For my Lord says *There's room enough,*
room enough in the heavens for us all,
My Lord says there's room enough,
Don't stay away.

2   Mourners, don't stay away,
> Mourners, don't stay away, ...
For the Bible says ...

3   Gambler, don't stay away,
> Gambler, don't stay away, ...
For the angels say ...

4   Sister, don't stay away,
> Sister, don't stay away ...
For Jesus says ...

(The New National Baptist Hymnal 1977, 491)

Prayer Focus: Lord, help me meditate day and night.

BIOY: Joshua 13-15 (62/303)

Exodus 13–14
"Don't You Let Nobody Turn You 'Round"

1   DON'T let nobody turn you aroun',
    Turn you roun', turn you roun',
    Don't let nobody turn you roun'
    Walking up the King's Highway.
2   Don't let ole Satan turn you aroun', ...
3   Don't let temptation turn you aroun', ...
4   Don't let no sinners turn you aroun', ...

(Walker 1979, 55)

Prayer Focus: Lord, if I could just hold my peace and let you fight my battles, then I know that victory shall be mine (Ex. 14:4,13–14)! If you could forever deliver the Israelites from the Egyptians, open up the Red Sea and swallow up mean ol' Pharaoh and his mighty army, then certainly you can deliver me. Walk with me Lord, on this highway to heaven, as you walked with the Israelites.

BIOY: Joshua 16-18 (63/302)

Psalm 2
"Done Foun' My Los' Sheep"

*DONE foun' my los' sheep, Done foun' my los'
sheep, Done foun' my los' sheep, (Hallelujah).
I done foun' my los' sheep, Done foun' my los'
sheep, Done foun' my los' sheep.*

1   My Lord a hundred sheep,
    One o' dem did go astray,
  That jes lef ' Him ninetyine;
    Go to de wilderness, seek an' fin',
  Ef you fin' min, bring him back,
    Cross de shoulders, Cross yo' back;
  Tell de neighbors all aroun',
    Dat los' sheep has done be foun'.

2   In dat Ressurrection Day sinner
    can't fin no hidin' place,
  Go to de mountain, de mountain move;
    Run to de hill, de hill run too,
  Sinner man trablin' on trembling groun',
    Po' los' sheep ain't nebber been foun',
  Sinner why don't yo' stop and pray,
    Den you'd hear de Shepherd say,
  *Done foun' my los' sheep, Done foun' my los'
  sheep, Done foun' my los' sheep.*

                    (Johnson and Johnson 1925, 167)

Prayer Focus: In thee, O Lord, do I put my trust.

BIOY: Joshua 19-21 (64/301)

DAY 65

Exodus 15-16
"Done wid Driber's Dribin'"

1 DONE wid driber's dribin',
   Done wid driber's dribin',
   Done wid driber's dribin',
   Roll, Jordan, roll.
2 Done wid massa's hollerin', ...
3 Done wid missus' scoldin', ...

(Southern 1997, 216)

Prayer Focus: Lord God, I thank and praise you for strong deliverance in my life. My heart sings and rejoices, for you have triumphed gloriously over my enemy. Sin and death are forever swallowed up in the Red Sea of your blood. I don't have to listen to the devil no more. You have set me free! My soul's been redeemed! I'm done with being abused by others and even by myself. No more lying, cheating, alcohol, drugs, gambling, and unholy living. Bread of Heaven, Bread of Heaven, feed me 'til I want no more.

BIOY: Joshua 22-24 (65/300)

Psalm 3
"Done With Sin and Sorrow"

OH! holy Lord! Oh! holy Lord! Oh! holy Lord!
Done with sin and sorrow.

1   Oh! rise up, children, get your crown,
     Done with sin and sorrow;
     And by your Savior's side sit down,
     Done with sin and sorrow.

2   O what a morning that will be, ...
     Our friends and Jesus we will see, ...

3   Oh, shout, you Christians,
     you're gaining ground, ...
     We'll shout old Satan's kingdom down, ...

4   I soon shall reach that golden shore, ...
     And sing the songs we sang before, ...

(Boatner and Townsend 1927, 38)

Prayer Focus: Deep down in the city of my soul there is
a hallelujah! Lord, please take me there.

BIOY: Judges 1-3 (66/299)

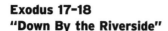

Exodus 17-18
"Down By the Riverside"

1   GOING to lay down my sword and shield,
Down by the riverside, down by the riverside,
down by the riverside,
Going to lay down my sword and shield,
Down by the riverside,
To study war no more;
I ain't goin' t' study war no more,
ain't goin' t' study war no more,
ain't goin' t' study war no more,
I ain't goin' t' study war no more,
ain't goin' t' study war no more,
ain't goin' t' study war no more.

2   Going to lay down my war shoes, ...

3   Going to put on my long white robe, ...

4   Going to meet my loving Savior, ...

(Boatner and Townsend 1927, 23)

Prayer Focus: Magnify my season of peace.

BIOY: Judges 4-6 (67/298)

Psalm 4
"Early in the Morning"

1   I MEET little Rosa early in de mornin',
    An I ax her, how you do my darter?
    O Jerusalem, early in de mornin';
        O Jerusalem, early in de mornin'.
    Walk 'em easy round de heaben,
        Walk 'em easy round de heaben,
    Walk 'em easy round de heaben,
        Till all living may join dat band. *

2   I meet my mudder early in de mornin';
    An' I ax her, how you do my mudder? …
3   I meet brudder Robert early in de mornin';
    I ax brudder Robert, how you do, my sonny? …
4   I meet titta-Wisa† early in de mornin';
    I ax titta-Wisa, how you do, my darter? …
                    (Allen, Ware, and Garrison 1867, 44)

   * O shout glory till 'em join dat ban'.
   † i.e., sister Louisa

Prayer Focus: Lord, early in the morning, while the dew is still on the roses, you give me joy.

BIOY: Judges 7–9 (68/297)

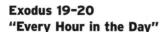

Exodus 19-20
"Every Hour in the Day"

ONE cold freezing morning lay dis body down;
I will pick up my cross an' follow my Lord
All roun' my Fader's throne.

1   Every hour in de day cry holy,
    Cry holy, my Lord!
    Every hour in de day cry holy,
    Oh show me de crime I've done.
2   Every hour in de night cry Jesus, ...

(Allen, Ware, and Garrison 1867, 58)

Prayer Focus: O Great and Holy One, I've sinned and fall short of your glory. I've broken your commandments. The penalty for my sin is death, yet your love for me is like pure gold and your gift to me is everlasting life through faith in Jesus Christ. My Lord, holy!

BIOY: Judges 10-13 (69/296)

Psalm 5
"Everytime I Feel the Spirit"

EV'RYTIME I feel the Spirit
Moving in my heart I will pray.

1 Jordan's river, chilly and cold,
  Chills the body, not the soul.
2 Upon the mountain my Lord spoke,
  Out His mouth came fire and smoke.
3 In the valley, on my knees,
  Ask my Lord have mercy, please.
4 All around me looks so shine,
  Ask my Lord if all is mine.

(Boatner and Townsend 1972, 27)

Prayer Focus: My Lord and my God, consider this meditation, lead me in your righteousness. Make your way straight before my face (Ps. 5:8).

BIOY: Judges 14-17 (70/295)

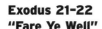

Exodus 21-22
"Fare Ye Well"

1   O FARE you well, my brudder,
     fare you well by de grace of God,
     For I'se gwinen home;
     I'se gwinen home, my Lord,
     I'se gwinen home.
2   Massa Jesus gib me a little broom,
     For to sweep my heart clean;
     Sweep 'em clean by de grace of God,
     An' glory in my soul.

(Allen, Ware, and Garrison 1867, 47)

Prayer Focus: Hear my prayer, O Lord, and give ear to my cry. Do not be silent at my tears, for I am a stranger with you, a sojourner, as all my foreparents were (Ps. 39:12; cf. Deut. 10:19). I'm glad to be alive. I miss those who have gone home; blessed be their memories. Now, give me grace to run this race.

BIOY: Judges 18-21 (71/294)

Psalm 6
"Father Abraham"

*FATHER Abraham sittin' down
    side ob de Holy Lam'.*

1 'Way up on-a de mountain top,
   My Lord he spoke an' chariot stop.
   Sittin' down, side ob de Holy Lam'
   Father Abraham,
   Sittin' down, side ob de Holy Lam'.

2 Good-bye mother an' fare you well,
   Meet me aroun' dat th'one ob God.
   Sittin' down, side ob de Holy Lam'
   Father Abraham,
   Sittin' down, side ob de Holy Lam'.

(Johnson and Johnson 1925, 144)

Prayer Focus: Great Advocate, hear the voice of my weeping. I am weary with groaning. All night I make my bed swim; I drench my couch with my tears. My eyes waste away because of grief. Receive my prayer. Let all my enemies be turned back and be ashamed.

BIOY: Ruth 1-2 (72/293)

Exodus 23-24
"Fix Me, Jesus"

OH, fix me; Oh, fix me; Oh, fix me;
fix me, Jesus, fix me.

1   Fix me for my long white robe
    Fix me, Jesus, fix me.
    Fix me for my starry crown.
    Fix me, Jesus, fix me.

2   Fix me for my journey home
    Fix me, Jesus, fix me.
    Fix me for my dying bed.
    Fix me, Jesus, fix me.

(Songs of Zion 1981, 122)

Prayer Focus: Not my brother, nor my sister, but it's me, O Lord, standing in the need of prayer!

BIOY: Ruth 3-4 (73/292)

Psalm 7
"Follow the Drinkin' Gourd"

1   FOLLOW the drinkin' gourd!
    Follow the drinkin' gourd.
    For the old man is a-wait-in'
    for to carry you to freedom
    If you follow the drinkin' gourd.
2   When the sun comes back
    and the first quail calls,
    Follow the drinkin' gourd.
    For the old man is a-wait-in'
    for to carry you to freedom
    If you follow the drinkin' gourd.

(Southern 1997, 145)

Prayer Focus: Merciful God, I will look unto heaven and follow the Bright and Morning Star. Break my bands and lead me out of darkness into an afternoon delight of freedom, truth, and life.

BIOY: 1 Samuel 1-4 (74/291)

DAY 75

Exodus 25-26
"Four and Twenty Elders"
(cf. Rev. 7:11-12)

1   SEE the four and twenty elders
    On their knees,
    See the four and twenty elders
    On their knees,
    And we'll all rise together
    And face the rising sun,
    O Lord have mercy, if you please.
2   They are bowing 'round the altar, ...
3   See Gideon's army bowing, ...
4   See Daniel in the den of lions, ...
5   Hebrew children in the fiery furnace, ...
6   We will praise our Lord together, ...

(Boatner and Townsend 1927, 70)

Prayer Focus: Blessings, glory, wisdom, thanksgiving, honor, power, and might be unto you!

BIOY: 1 Samuel 5-7 (75/290)

Psalm 8
"Free at Last"

FREE at last, free at last,
Thank God a' mighty I'm free at last.

1 Surely been 'buked and surely been scorned,
   Thank God a'mighty, I'm free at last.
   But still my soul is a heaven born,
   Thank God a'mighty, I'm free at last.

2 If you don't know that I been redeemed,
   Thank God a'mighty, I'm free at last.
   Just follow me down to Jordan's stream,
   Thank God a'mighty, I'm free at last.

(Songs of Zion 1981, 80)

Prayer Focus: Let justice run down like water and righteousness like a mighty stream (Amos 5:24).

BIOY: 1 Samuel 8-11 (76/289)

Exodus 27-28
"Freedom Train a-Comin'"

1 HEAR that a freedom train a coming,
      coming, coming,
  Hear that freedom train a coming,
      coming , coming,
  Hear that freedom train a coming,
      coming, coming,
  Get on board, oh, oh, get on board.

2 It'll be carryin' nothing but freedom,
      freedom, freedom, ...
  Get on board, oh, oh, get on board.

3 They'll be comin' by the thousand,
      thousand, thousand, ...
  Get on board, oh, oh, get on board.

4 It'll be carryin' freedom fighters,
      fighters, fighters, ...
  Get on board, oh, oh, get on board.

5 It'll be carryin' registered voters,
      voters, voters, ...
  Get on board, oh, oh, get on board.

6 It'll be rollin' through Mississippi,
      Mississippi, Mississippi, ...
  Get on board, oh, oh, get on board.

(Songs of Zion 1981, 92)

Prayer Focus: Help me board freedom's soul train.

BIOY: 1 Samuel 12-14 (77/288)

Psalm 9
"Get Right With God"

GET right with God, and do it now;
Get right with God, and He will show you how,
*   (hallelujah!)*
Down at the cross, where He shed His blood,
Get right with God, get right, get right with God.

1   Jesus Christ my King, He is all to me;
    He blest my heart, and gives me ev'rything;
    Living by His word, He is in my soul;
    Down at the cross, get right, get right with God.

2   He's working now, down in my heart;
    He is sweet to me, O what pleasure I fine;
    He is the living way, come, and hear Him say, …

4   Lord, come the more, me your favors show;
    Lord, let me know which way to go;
    Come in my heart, filling every part, …

                          (Boatner and Townsend 1927, 51)

Prayer Focus: Lord, I want to be right with you.

BIOY: 1 Samuel 15-17 (78/287)

◙◙◙◙◙◙◙◙◙◙◙◙◙◙◙◙◙◙◙◙◙◙◙◙◙◙◙

Exodus 29-30
"Gimme Dat Ol' Time Religion"

GIMME dat ol' time religion,
gimme dat ol' time religion,
gimme dat ol' time religion,
It's good enough for me.

1   It was good for de Hebrew children,
    it was good for de Hebrew children,
    it was good for de Hebrew children,
    An' it's good enough for me.

2   It will do when de world's on fi-ah,
    it will do when de world's on fi-ah,
    it will do when de world's on fi-ah,
    An' it's good enough for me.

(Johnson and Johnson 1925, 76)

Prayer Focus: Certainly, certainly, certainly Lord, it's good enough for me! I wouldn't have a religion that I couldn't feel sometime. Touch me, Jesus.

BIOY: 1 Samuel 18-20 (79/286)

Psalm 10
"Gimme Yo' Han'"

O, GIMME yo' han', Gimme yo' han',
All I want is de love o' God;
Gimme yo' han', gimme yo' han',
You mus' be lovin' at God's comman'.

1 You say you're aimin' for de skies,
   You mus' be lovin' at God's comman'
   Why don't you quit yo' tellin' lies,
   You mus' be lovin' at God's comman'.

2 You say de Lord has set you free, ...
   Why don't you let yo' neighbor be, ...

3 Some seek God's grace but don't seek right, ...
   Dey pray in de day, but none at night, ...

(Johnson and Johnson 1926, 86)

Prayer Focus: Lord, you hear the desires of the humble. Do justice to the oppressed that the oppressor may persecute no more (Ps. 10:17–18).

BIOY: 1 Samuel 21-24 (80/285)

Exodus 31-32
"So Glad I Done Got Over"

SO glad, (I) Done got over,
So glad, (I) Done got over,
So glad, (I) Done got over,
Done got over at last.

1 Satan's mad and I'm so glad,
   (I) Done got over at last,
   He missed that soul that he thought he had,
   (I) Done got over at last.

(Mt. Tabor MBC, Track 2)

Prayer Focus: Lord, the road was rough, the going was tough, but I made it. Lord, so many naysayers said I wouldn't make it but, because of your goodness and mercy, I done got over! Praise God!

BIOY: 1 Samuel 25-27 (81/284)

Psalm 11
"Give Me Jesus"
(cf. Mark 8:36)

1   OH, when I come to die, Oh, when I come to die,
    Oh, when I come to die, *Give me Jesus.*
    In dat mornin' when I rise,
        Dat mornin' when I rise,
    In dat mornin' when I rise, *Give me Jesus.*
    Give me Jesus, give me Jesus,
    You may have all dis worl', give me Jesus,
    Oh give me Jesus, give me Jesus,
    You may have all dis worl', give me Jesus.
2   Dark midnight was my cry,
        Dark midnight was my cry,
    Dark midnight was my cry, …
    I heard a mourner say, I heard a mourner say,
    I heard a mourner say, …

                    (Johnson and Johnson 1925, 160)

Prayer Focus: I choose you, Jesus; I trust you!

BIOY: 1 Samuel 28-31 (82/283)

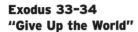

Exodus 33-34
"Give Up the World"

1 DE sun give a light* in de heaven all round,
  De sun give a light in de heaven all round,
  De sun give a light in de heaven all round,
  Why don't you give up de world?
2 My brudder, don't you give up de world?
  My brudder, don't you give up de world?
  My brudder, don't you give up de world?
  We must leave de world behind.

(Allen, Ware, and Garrison 1867, 27)

* De moon give a light, de starry crown, ...

Prayer Focus: You say that we are a stiff-necked people, and rightfully so. I apologize for doing you wrong after all you've done for me. Give me one more chance; I want to start anew. In thee, O Lord, do I put my trust.

BIOY: 2 Samuel 1-3 (83/282)

Psalm 12
"Glory, Glory, Hallelujah"

GLORY, glory, hallelujah!
When I lay my burden down,
Glory, glory, hallelujah!
When I lay my burden down.

1   If I had died when I was young,
     When I lay my burden down,
    I never would had dis race to run,
     When I lay my burden down.

2   One day, one day I walked along, ...
    The Elements open an' der love come down, ...

3   Oh, since I left ole Satan's field, ...
    I have carried God's burning zeal, ...

                   (Boatner and Townsend 1927, 3)

Prayer Focus: Your words are pure, like silver tried in a furnace of earth, purified seven times.

BIOY: 2 Samuel 4-6 (84/281)

DAY 85

Exodus 35-36
"Go in the Wilderness"

I WAIT upon de Lord, I wait upon de Lord,
I wait upon de Lord, my God, who take away de
sin of the world.

1   If you want to find Jesus, go in the wilderness,
    Go in de wilderness, go in de wilderness,
    Mournin' brudder, go in de wilderness,
    I wait upon de Lord.

3   You want to be a Christian, …

4   You want to get religion, …

5   If you spec' to be converted, …

    …

9   Half-done Christian, …

10 Come backslider, …

(Allen, Ware, and Garrison 1867, 14)

Prayer Focus: I welcome you to the tabernacle that is in me.

BIOY: 2 Samuel 7-10 (85/280)

Psalm 13
"Go, Tell It on the Mountain"

GO, tell it on the mountain,
Over the hills and everywhere,
Go, tell it on the mountain
That Jesus Christ is born.

1 While shepherds kept their watching,
O'er silent flocks by night,
Behold throughout the heavens
There shone a holy light.

2 The shepherds feared and trembled,
When lo! above the earth,
Rang out the angel chorus
That hailed our Savior's birth.

3 Down in a lowly manger,
The humble Christ was born,
And God sent us salvation
That blessed Christmas morn.

(Songs of Zion 1981, 75)

Prayer Focus: How long, O Lord? Do not forget me (Ps. 13:1).

BIOY: 2 Samuel 11-14 (86/279)

Exodus 37-38
"God Got Plenty O' Room"

GOD got plenty o' room, got plenty o' room,
'Way in de kingdom,
God got plenty o' room my Jesus say,
'Way in de kingdom.

1   Brethren, I have come again,
    'Way in de kingdom,
    To help you all to pray and sing,
    'Way in de kingdom.

2   So many-a weeks and days have passed, ...
    Since we met together last, ...

3   Old Satan tremble when he sees, ...
    The weakest saints upon their knees, ...

4   Prayer makes the darkest cloud withdraw, ...
    Prayer climbed the ladder Jacob saw, ...

5   John's divine communion feel, ...
    Joseph's meek and Joshua's zeal, ...

                    (Allen, Ware, and Garrison 1867, 106)

Prayer Focus: I pray there is still room for me in the kingdom.

BIOY: 2 Samuel 15-18 (87/278)

Psalm 14
"God Is a God"

GOD is a God!
God don't never change!
God is a God
An' He always will be God!

1 He made the sun to shine by day,
   He made the sun to show the way,
   He made the stars to show their light,
   He made the moon to shine by night (saying) …

2 The earth His foot-stool an' heav'n His throne,
   The whole creation all His own,
   His love an' power will prevail,
   His promises will never fail (saying) …

(Songs of Zion 1981, 140)

Prayer Focus: Only a fool utters from the heart, "There is no God." But as for me, I know that you are real; for I can feel you deep within. I love you, Lord.

BIOY: 2 Samuel 19-20 (88/277)

Exodus 39-40
"God's a-Gwinter Trouble de Water"
(cf. John 5:4)

WADE in de water, children,
*   Wade in de water, children,*
Wade in de water, children,
*   God's gwinter trouble de water.*

1 See dat host all dressed in white,
   God's a-gwinter trouble de water;
   De leader looks like de Israelite,
   God's a-gwinter trouble de water.

2 See dat ban' all dressed in red,
   God's a-gwinter trouble de water;
   Looks like de ban' dat Moses lead,
   God's a-gwinter trouble de water.

(Johnson and Johnson 1926, 84)

Prayer Focus: Lord, wash me, clean me, sanctify me. Purge me with thy hyssop of heavenly blood.

BIOY: 2 Samuel 21-22 (89/276)

Psalm 15
"God's Goin' to Straighten Them"

WE got deacons* in de church,
Dey ain't straight,
Who's goin' to straighten them?
God's goin' to straighten them,
He says He's goin' to straighten them,
God's goin' to straighten
    all de people in His church.

(Lovell 1972, 339)

* [preachers, members]

Prayer Focus: Lord, you are merciful and gracious, long-suffering, and abounding in goodness and truth. You keep mercy for thousands, forgiving iniquity, transgression and sin. You by no means clear the guilty, but visit the iniquity of the fathers upon the children to the third and fourth generation (Ex. 34:6–7). May I abide in your tabernacle?

BIOY: 2 Samuel 23-24 (90/275)

Leviticus 1-2
"God's Going to Set This World on Fire"

1   GOD'S going to set this world on fire,
     God's going to set this world on fire,
     Some of these days, Hallelujah!
     God's going to set this world on fire,
     God's going to set this world on fire,
     Some of these days.

2   I'm going to sit at the welcome table, …

3   I'm going to eat and won't be hungry, …

4   I'm going to drink and won't be thirsty, …

(Boatner and Townsend 1927, 4)

Prayer Focus: I have longed for sweet peace and for faith to increase; to this end have earnestly, fervently prayed. Lord, my all on the altar of sacrifice I lay. My heart, Holy Spirit, do control. I want to be blessed and have peace and sweet rest. I yield to you my body and soul (mind, emotions, will).

BIOY: 1 Kings 1-4 (91/274)

Psalm 16
"Good News"

GOOD news, (Good news) The Chariot's coming,
Good news, (Good news) The Chariot's coming,
Good news, (Good news) The Chariot's coming,
An' I don't want you to leave me behind.

1   There are long white robes in the heavens, I know,
    There are long white robes in the heavens, I know,
    There are long white robes in the heavens, I know,
    And I don't want you to leave me behind.

2   There are starry crowns in the heavens, I know, ...

3   There are silver slippers in the heavens, I know, ...

(Boatner and Townsend 1927, 29)

Prayer Focus: Preserve me, O God, for in you I put my trust. Do not leave my soul in Sheol nor let me see corruption. Show me the path of life. Swing low, sweet chariot, and take me home to pleasures forevermore.

BIOY: 1 Kings 5-8 (92/273)

Leviticus 3-4
"Good News, Member"

GOOD news, member, good news, member,
Don't you mind what Satan say;
Good news, member, good news,
And I hearde from heav'n today.

1 My brudder have a seat and I so glad,
   Good news, member, good news;
   My brudder have a seat and I so glad,
   And I hearde from heav'n today.
2 Mr. Hawley have a home in Paradise, ...
3 Archangel bring baptizing down, ...

(Allen, Ware, and Garrison 1867, 97)

Prayer Focus: Heaven has thus spoken: the sacrifices
that you require of me are a broken spirit and a contrite
heart (Ps. 51:17). These I gladly give.

BIOY: 1 Kings 9-11 (93/272)

DAY 94

Psalm 17
"Good-bye"

GOOD-BYE, my brudder, good-bye, Hallelujah!
Good-bye, sister Sally, good-bye, Hallelujah!
Going home, Hallelujah!
Jesus call me, Hallelujah!
Linger no longer, Hallelujah!
Tarry no longer, Hallelujah!

(Allen, Ware, and Garrison 1867, 52)

Prayer Focus: Incline your ear to my cry, O God. Show your marvelous lovingkindness to me. Save me from those who rise up against me. Keep me as the apple of your eye. Hide me under the shadow of your wings from the wicked who oppress me.

BIOY: 1 Kings 12-14 (94/271)

Leviticus 5-6
"Good-bye, Brother"

1   GOOD-BYE, brother, good-bye,
    If I don't see you more;
    Now God bless you, now God bless you,
    If I don't see you more.

2   We part in de body but we meet in de spirit, ...
    We'll meet in de heaben in de blessed* kingdom.

3   So good-bye, brother, good-bye, sister; ...
    Now God bless you, now God bless you.

             (Allen, Ware, and Garrison 1867, 47)

  * Glorious

Prayer Focus: Oh, God! The forceful and violent attack on the family unit was and is a sorrowful, traumatic, tragedy. Constant heartache and deep, unrelenting pain; such misery! Thank God there is no sorrow on earth that heaven can not heal!

BIOY: 1 Kings 15-18 (95/270)

Psalm 18
"Great Day"

GREAT day!
Great day, de righteous marchin', Great day!
God's gwinter build up Zion's walls.

1   De chariot rode on de mountain top,
    God's gwinter build up Zion's walls,
    My God He spoke an' de chariot stop,
    God's gwinter build up Zion's walls.

2   Dis is de day of jubilee, ...
    De Lord has set his people free, ...

3   Gwine take my breas'plate, sword in han', ...
    An' march out boldly, in-a de field, ...

4   We want no cowards in our ban', ...
    We call for valiant hearted men, ...

(Johnson and Johnson 1926, 56)

Prayer Focus: Blessed God of my salvation—my strength, my deliverer, my stronghold—be exalted!

BIOY: 1 Kings 19-22 (96/269)

Leviticus 7-8
"Gwine Follow"

TITTY Mary, you know I gwine follow,
I gwine to follow, gwine follow,
Brudder William, you know I gwine to follow,
For to do my Fader will.
'Tis well and good I'm a-comin' here tonight,
I'm a-comin' here tonight,
I'm a-comin' here tonight.
'Tis well and good, I'm a-comin' here tonight,
For to do my Fader will.

(Allen, Ware, and Garrison 1967, 18)

Prayer Focus: Lord God, anoint me and sanctify me to do your will. Because obedience is better than sacrifice (1 Sam. 15:22; Prov. 21:3), I will wait until your Spirit comes, then move at your command.

BIOY: 2 Kings 1-3 (97/268)

Psalm 19
"Gwine Up"

OH, yes, I'm gwine up, gwine up,
gwine all de way, Lord
Gwine up, gwine up, to see de heabenly lan'.

1 Oh, Saints an' sinners will-a you go,
   See de heabenly lan',
   I'm a gwine up to heab'n fo' to see my robe,
   See de heabenly lan';
   Gwine to see my robe an' try it on,
   See de habenly lan',
   It am brighter dan-a dat glitterin' sun,
   See de heabenly lan'.

2 Oh, gwine to keep a climin' high, ...
   Till I meet dem-a angels in-a de sky, ...
   Dem-a snow white angels I shall see, ...
   Den de debbil am-a gwine to let-a me be, ...
                            (Johnson and Johnson 1925, 118)

Prayer Focus: Cleanse me from secret faults.

BIOY: 2 Kings 4-5 (98/267)

DAY 99

Leviticus 9-10
"Gwinter Ride Up in de Chariot Soon-a in de Mornin'"

1   GWINTER ride up in de chariot,
         Soon-a in de mornin'
     Ride up in de chariot, *Soon-a in de mornin'*
     Ride up in de chariot, *Soon-a in de mornin'*
     An' I hope I'll jine de ban'.
     O, Lord, have mercy on me,
     O, Lord, have mercy on me,
     O, Lord, have mercy on me,
     An' I hope I'll jine de ban'.
2   (Gwinter) Meet my brother dere, yes, ...
3   (Gwinter) Chatter wid de angels, ...
4   (Gwinter) Meet my Massa Jesus, ...
5   (Gwinter) Walk and talk wid Jesus, ...

(Johnson and Johnson 1926, 121)

Prayer Focus: O Lord have mercy on me! Help me to discern between the holy and the unholy. Teach me your statutes.

BIOY: 2 Kings 6-8 (99/266)

Psalm 20
"Gwinter Sing all Along de Way"

OH, I'm a gwinter sing, gwinter sing,
gwinter sing all along de way,
Oh, I'm a gwinter sing, gwinter sing,
gwinter sing all along de way.

1 We'll raise de Christians' banner,
  the motto's new an' old,
  Repentance an' salvation,
  Am graven dere in gold.

2 We'll shout o'er our sorrows,
  An' sing forever more,
  With Christ an' all his army,
  On dat celestial shore.

(Johnson and Johnson 1925, 128)

Prayer Focus: Lord, answer me in the day of trouble. Send me help from your sanctuary.

BIOY: 2 Kings 9–12 (100/265)

Leviticus 11–12
"Hail, Mary"

1   I WANT some valiant soldier here,
    I want some valiant soldier here,
    I want some valiant soldier here,
    To help me bear de cross.

2   O hail, Mary, hail!
    O hail, Mary, hail!
    O hail, Mary, hail!
    To help me bear de cross.

(Allen, Ware, and Garrison 1867, 45)

Prayer Focus: Lord, hold my hand while I run this race. I don't want to race this race in vain. Lord, I'm running, trying to make one hundred—ninety-nine and one half won't do. Why don't you help me run this race? I don't want to run this race in vain. Save now, I pray, O Lord. O Lord, I pray, send now prosperity (Ps. 118:25). Send help now!

BIOY: 2 Kings 13–15 (101/264)

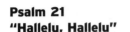

Psalm 21
"Hallelu, Hallelu"

1   OH one day as an oder, Hallelu, hallelu!
2   When de ship is out a sailin', Hallelujah!
3   Member walk and never tire.
4   Member walk Jordan long road.
5   Member walk tribulation.
6   You go home to Wappoo.
7   Member seek new repentance.
8   I go to seek my fortune.
9   I go to seek my dying Saviour.
10 You want to die like Jesus.

(Allen, Ware, and Garrison 1867, 50)

Prayer Focus: Be exalted, O Lord! My heart sings and praises your holiness! Your law is perfect, converting the soul. Your testimony is sure, making wise the simple. Your statutes are right, rejoicing the heart. Your commandments pure, enlightening the eyes. Your judgments true and righteous altogether.

BIOY: 2 Kings 16-19 (102/263)

Leviticus 13–14
"Hallelujah!"

HALLELUJAH! an' a hallelujah!
Hallelujah, Lord! I been down into the sea.
1. O, I've been to de sea an' I've been tried,
   Been down into the sea;
   O, I've been to de sea an' I've been baptize',
   Been down into the sea.
2. O, Christians, Can't you rise an' tell, …
   The glories of Immanuel? …
3. If, you don't b'lieve I've been redeemed, …
   Watch my face for the gospel gleam, …
4. I'm born of God, I know I am, …
   I'm purchased by the dying Lamb, …

(Johnson and Johnson 1925, 172)

Prayer Focus: I am so wondrously saved from sin! Glory to your name! Praise God! Hallelujah!

Psalm 22
"Happy Morning"

WEEP no more, Marta,
Weep no more, Mary,*
Jesus rise from de dead,
Happy† morning.

Glorious‡ morning,
Glorious morning,
My Saviour rise from de dead,
Happy morning.

(Allen, Ware, and Garrison 1867, 10)

* Doubt no more, Thomas.
† Glorious, Sunday.
‡ O what a happy Sunday.

Prayer Focus: Lord, you arose, you arose, you arose from the dead. I know you shall bear my spirit home so that where you are I may also be.

BIOY: 2 Kings 23-25 (104/261)

DAY 105

Leviticus 15-16
"Hard Trials"

1   THE foxes, they have holes in the ground,
    The birds have nests in the air,
    The Christians have a hiding place,
    But sinners ain't got nowhere.
    Now ain't them hard trials, great tribulations?
    Ain't them hard trials?
      I'm bound to leave this land.

2   Oh, Methodist, Methodist is my name,
    Methodist till I die,
    Been baptized on the Methodist side,
    And a Methodist will I die.

3   Oh, Baptist, Baptist is my name,
    Baptist till I die,
    Been baptized on the Baptist side,
    And a Baptist will I die.

(Songs of Zion 1981, 107)

Prayer Focus: I worship you in spirit and in truth.

BIOY: 1 Chronicles 1-3 (105/260)

Psalm 23
"He Arose"

1   THEY crucified my Savior
and nailed Him to the cross, (3 times)
And the Lord shall bear my spirit home.
He arose, He arose,
He arose from the dead, (3x)
And the Lord shall bear my spirit home.

2   Joseph begged His body
and laid it in the tomb, (3x)
And the Lord shall bear my spirit home.

3   Mary, she came running
a-looking for my Lord, (3x)
And the Lord shall bear my spirit home.

4   An angel came from heaven
and rolled the stone away, (3x)
And the Lord shall bear my spirit home.

                             (Boatner and Townsend 1927, 56)

Prayer Focus: Precious Lord, you are awesome!

BIOY: 1 Chronicles 4–6 (106/259)

DAY 107

Leviticus 17-18
"He Never Said a Mumbalin' Word"

1 THEY crucified my Lord,
   and he never said a mumbalin' word;
   they crucified my Lord,
   and he never said a mumbalin' word,
   not a word, not a word, not a word.

2 They nailed him to the tree, ...
   they nailed him to the tree, ...

3 They pierced him in the side, ...
   they pierced him in the side, ...

4 His blood came trickling down, ...
   his blood came trickling down, ...

5 He hung his head and died, ...
   he hung his head and died, ...

   (The AME Bicentennial Hymnal 1996, 155)

Prayer Focus: They whipped, beat, and mocked you, then hung you on a tree to die. Yes, you understand my pain, the pain of my people, and what it means to be black in America!

BIOY: 1 Chronicles 7-9 (107/258)

DAY 108

Psalm 24
"He's Got His Eyes on Me"

1 I WOULD not be a sinner,
   I'll tell you the reason why,
   O, my Lord, sitting in the kingdom,
   He's got His eyes on me.
   He's got His eyes on me, my Lord,
   He's got His eyes on me, my Lord,
   O, my Lord, sitting in the kingdom,
   He's got His eyes on me.

2 I would not be a pretender, ...

3 I would not be a sland'rer, ...

4 I would not be a hypocrite, ...

5 I would not be a deceiver, ...

(Boatner and Townsend 1927, 60)

Prayer Focus: Your eyes look from heaven. You watch my secret sins. Lord, have mercy on me.

BIOY: 1 Chronicles 10-13 (108/257)

DAY 109

Leviticus 19-20
"He's Got the Whole World in His Hand"

1   HE'S got the whole world in His hand,
He's got the whole world in His hand,
He's got the whole world in His hand,
He's got the whole world in His hand.

2   He's got all power in His hand,
He's got all power in His hand,
He's got all power in His hand,
He's got the whole world in His hand.

3   He's got my mother in His hand, (x3)
He's got the whole world in His hand.

4   He's got my father in His hand, (x3)
He's got the whole world in His hand.

5   He's got the fishes of the sea in His hand, (x3) …

6   He's got the whole church in His hand, (x3) …

(Boatner and Townsend 1927, 68)

Prayer Focus: Precious Lord, take my hand. I want to put my hand in the hand of the Man who made the skies and the sea—the One from Galilee!

BIOY: 1 Chronicles 14-16 (109/256)

෦෮෮෮෮෮෮෮෮෮෮෮෮෮෮෮෮෮෮෮෮෮෮෮෮෮෮෮

Psalm 25
"He's Jus' de Same Today" (John 8:58)

1 WHEN Moses an' his soldiers,
    f'om Egypt's lan' did flee,
His enemies were in behin' him,
    An' in front of him de sea.
God raised de waters like a wall,
    An' opened up de way,
An' de God dat lived in Moses' *time*
    is jus' de same today.
Is jus' de same today, Jus' de same today,
An' de God dat lived in Moses' time
    is jus' de same today.
2 When Daniel faithful to his God,
    would not bow to men,
An' by God's enemy he was hurled into de lions den.
God locked de lion's jaw we read,
    An' robbed him of his prey,
An' de God dat lived in Daniel's *time*
    is jus' de same today.

                        (Johnson and Johnson 1925, 80)

Prayer Focus: O mighty Creator, ruler of the heavens and the earth: across the years, through the generations, you are always the same. Hallelujah! (Ps. 102:25–27; Heb. 13:8)

BIOY: 1 Chronicles 17–20 (110/255)

Leviticus 21-22
"Hear Me Praying"

LORD, oh, hear me praying, Lord,
   oh, hear me praying,
Lord, oh, hear me praying;
   I want to be more holy ev'ry day.

1   Like Peter when you said to him, Feed my sheep,
    Like Peter when you said to him, feed my sheep,
    Like Peter when you said to him, Feed my lambs,
    Like Peter when you said to him, feed my lambs.

2   Like Peter when you said to him, I build my church,
    Like Peter when you said to him, upon this rock,
    Like Peter when you said to him, The gates of hell
    Like Peter when you said to him, will never shock.

3   Like the Baptist when you said, I am a voice,
    Like the Baptist when you said, crying ev'ry day,
    Like the Baptist when you said, In the wilderness,
    Like the Baptist when you said, "Prepare the way."
                    (The New National Baptist Hymnal 1977, 487)

Prayer Focus: Lord, oh, hear me pray today!

BIOY: 1 Chronicles 21-23 (111/254)

Psalm 26
"Heav'n Boun' Soldier"

HOLD out yo' light you heav'n boun' soldier,
Hold out yo' light you heav'n boun' soldier,
Hold out yo' light you heav'n boun' soldier,
Let yo' light shine aroun' de world.

1 O, deacon can't yo' hold out yo' light,
   O, deacon can't yo' hold out yo' light,
   O, deacon can't yo' hold out yo' light,
   Let yo' light shine aroun' de world.

2 O, preacher can't yo' hold out yo' light,
   O, preacher can't yo' hold out yo' light,
   O, preacher can't yo' hold out yo' light,
   Let yo' light shine aroun' de world.

(Johnson and Johnson 1925, 54)

Prayer Focus: Lord, this little light of mine, I am going to let it shine, let it shine, let it shine, let it shine!

BIOY: 1 Chronicles 24–26 (112/253)

Leviticus 23-24
"I Know It Was the Blood"

1   I KNOW it was the blood,
I know it was the blood,
I know it was the blood *for me,*
One day when I was lost,
Jesus died on the cross,
I know it was the blood *for me.*

2   It was my Savior's blood ...

3   The blood came streaming down ...

4   He suffered, bled, and died ...

5   I know He's coming back ...

(Warren 1997, 56)

Prayer Focus: Lord, I thank you for the Sabbath, a time of rest, a time of worship, a time to reflect on such things as: who and whose I am; where I've been, am, and am going; the price paid for my freedom; and the power in my Savior's blood.

Psalm 27
"Heaven Bell a-Ring"

1 MY Lord, my Lord, what shall I do?
   And a heav'n bell a-ring and praise God.
   Timmy, Timmy, orphan boy.
   Robert, Robert, orphan child.
2 What shall I do for a hiding place?...
3 I run to de sea, but de sea run dry, ...
4 I run to de gate, but de gate shut fast, ...
5 No hiding place for sinner dere, ...
6 Say you when you get to heaven
   say you 'member me, ...
7 Your righteous Lord shall find you out, ...
8 He cast out none dat come by faith, ...
9 You look to de Lord wid a tender heart, ...
10 Say Christmas come but once a year, ...
11 Say Sunday come but once a week, ...

(Allen, Ware, and Garrison 1867, 20)

Prayer Focus: Lord, you are my light and my salvation; whom shall I fear? Whom shall I fear!

BIOY: 2 Chronicles 1–4 (114/251)

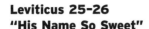

Leviticus 25-26
"His Name So Sweet"

OH Lawd, I jes come from de fountain,
I'm jes from de fountain, Lawd,
Jes come from de fountain,
His name so sweet.

1   Po' sinnuh, do you love Jesus?
    Yes, yes, I do love mah Jesus.
    Sinnuh, do you love Jesus?
    His name so sweet.
2   Class leader, do you love Jesus? …
3   'Sidin' elder, do you love Jesus? …
                              (Songs of Zion 1981, 90)

Prayer Focus: Jesus, I love to hear your name! It gives me strength to carry on. Just the sound of your name soothes my doubts and calms my fears. It's sweeter also than honey and the honeycomb.

BIOY: 2 Chronicles 5-7 (115/250)

Psalm 28
"Hol' de Win' Don't Let It Blow"

HOL' de win'! Hol' de win'!
Hol' de win' don't let it blow;
Hol' de win'! Hol' de win'!
Hol' de win' don't let it blow.

1 Talk about me jes' as much as you please,
   Hol' de win' don't let it blow;
   De more you talk I'm gwinter ben' my knees,
   Hol' de win' don't let it blow.

2 You ask me why I kin shout-a so bol', ...
   De love of Jesus sho' is in my soul, ...

3 You ask me why I am always so glad, ...
   De devil missed de soul he tho't he had, ...

4 I'm gwine to heab'n an' I'm gwine dere right, ...
   I'm gwine to heab'n all a dressed in white, ...

(Johnson and Johnson 1926, 178)

Prayer Focus: Going to heaven: that's what I'm talking about!

BIOY: 2 Chronicles 8-10 (116/249)

Leviticus 27
"Hold On"

KEEP yo' han' on de plow,
Hold on! Hold on!
Hold on! Hold on!

1   Nora, Nora, let me come in,
    Do' s' all fast'ned an' de winders pinned,

2   Nora said, "Ya lost yo' track,
    Can' plow straight an' keep a lookin' back,"

3   If you wanna get to Heaven, let me tell you how:
    Jus' keep yo' han' on de gospel plow,

4   If dat plow stays in yo' han'
    It'll lan' you straight into de promised lan'.

(Songs of Zion 1981, 86)

Prayer Focus: Lord, we are soldiers in your army. We have to fight, although we may have to cry sometimes. We've got to hold up your blood-stained banner. We've got to hold on to the gospel plow and fight until we die!

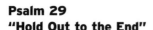

Psalm 29
"Hold Out to the End"

ALL dem Mount Zion member,
dey have many ups and downs;
But cross come or no come,
for to hold out to the end.
Hold out to the end,
hold out to the end,
It is my 'termination for to
hold out to the end.

(Allen, Ware, and Garrison 1867, 57)

Prayer Focus: Lord I give unto you glory and honor. I worship you in the beauty of holiness. You are the God of glory—all powerful and full of majesty. Give strength to your people and bless them with strength. Strengthen me that I may press on the upward way to new heights, hold on to my faith, and see what the end may be.

BIOY: 2 Chronicles 14-16 (118/247)

Numbers 1-2
"Hold Your Light"

WHAT make ole Satan da follow me so?
Satan hain't nottin' at all for to do wid* me.
    (Run seeker.)
Hold your light, (Sister Mary,†)
Hold your light, (Seeker turn back,)
Hold your light on Canaan shore.

(Allen, Ware, and Garrison 1867, 10)

* Long o'
† All de member, Turn seeker

Prayer Focus: Lord God, you say that Satan, like a fearful snake in the grass trying to bite me as I pass, is full of deceit. By your grace and power, deliver me from the wiles of the evil one. Equip me with godly armor, and guide me safely to freedom's shore.

Psalm 30
"Holy Bible" (2 Pet. 1:20-21)

HOLY Bible, Holy Bible,
Holy Bible, book divine, book divine—
Before I'd be a slave,
I'd be buried in my grave,
And go home to my Father and be saved.

(Lovell 1972, 263)

Prayer Focus: Lord, you say that all Scripture is given by inspiration of you, and is profitable for doctrine, for reproof, for correction, for instruction in righteousness, that I may be complete, thoroughly equipped for every good work (2 Tim. 3:16–17). I'm changing. I'm striving to do better, to do your will, and to study your Word (2 Tim. 2:15). I find that living this life according to your Word pierces my soul (Heb. 4:12). I'm learning that weeping endures but a night; joy comes in the morning (Ps. 30:5)!

BIOY: 2 Chronicles 21-24 (120/245)

◎◎◎◎◎◎◎◎◎◎◎◎◎◎◎◎◎◎◎◎◎◎◎◎◎◎◎◎◎◎

Numbers 3-4
"Humble Yo'self de Bell Done Ring"

LIVE-A humble, humble, Lord;
  Humble yo'self, de bell done ring. (2x)
Glory an' honor! Praise King Jesus!
Glory an' honor! Praise de Lord! (2x)
Oh, my young Christians I got lots for to tell you,
Jesus Christ speakin' thro' de organs of de clay.
  ("One day, one day, Lord!")
God's gwinter call dem chillun f'om a distant lan'.
Tombstones a-crackin' graves a-bustin'
Hell an' de sea an gwinter give up de dead.
False pretender wears sheep clothin' on his back,
In his heart he's like a ravin' wolf.
  ("Judge ye not, brother,")
For yet shall be judged false pretender
  gettin in de Christian band.
Watch dat sun how steady he run,
Don't let him catch you wid yo' work undone.
Ever see such a man as God?
He gave up his son, for to come an' die;
Gave up his son, for to come an' die,
  jus' to save my soul from a burnin' fire....
  (Johnson and Johnson 1926, 183)

Prayer Focus: Help me to live humble and holy.

BIOY: 2 Chronicles 25-26 (121/244)

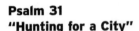

Psalm 31
"Hunting for a City"

I AM huntin' for a city,
to stay awhile,
I am huntin' for a city,
to stay awhile,
I am huntin' for a city,
to stay awhile,
O believer got a home at las.

(Allen, Ware, and Garrison 1867, 18)

Prayer Focus: "Blessed be the Lord, For He has shown me His marvelous kindness in a strong city!" (Ps. 31:21). Oh, how great is your goodness, which you have laid up for those who fear you in the presence of others. Hide me in the secret place of your presence from the plots of the evil one and his servants. Keep me secretly in a pavilion from the strife of gossiping tongues (cf. Ps. 31:19–20). In thee, O Lord, I put my trust. Guide me through life's storms.

BIOY: 2 Chronicles 27-28 (122/243)

Numbers 5-6
"Hunting for the Lord" (Acts 17:26-28)

HUNT till you find him,
Hallelujah,
And a huntin' for de Lord;
Till you find him,
Hallelujah,
And a huntin' for de Lord.

(Allen, Ware, and Garrison 1867, 13)

Prayer Focus: "And those who know Your name will put their trust in You; For You, Lord, have not forsaken those who seek You" (Ps. 9:10). Lord, you have promised in your Word that those who seek you will find you (cf. Deut. 4:29). I thank you, for you are near to all who call upon you in truth (Ps. 145:17). I'm calling on you, Master. Have mercy on me, O Lord, for I am in trouble. Fear is on every side. Deliver me from the hands of my enemies and from those who persecute me (Ps. 31:9–15).

BIOY: 2 Chronicles 29-32 (123/242)

Psalm 32
"Hush! Hush! Amen"

HUSH! hush! somebody calls my name;
Hush! hush! somebody calls my name;
Hush! hush! somebody calls my name;
Halleluia, Amen.

1   Christ said, Nicodemus, you must be born again, ...
    Halleluia, Amen.
2   How can a man be born when he's old? ...
    Halleluia, Amen.
3   Just believe, repent, and be baptized, ...
    Halleluia, Amen.

(Boatner and Townsend 1927, 64)

Prayer Focus: I acknowledge my sin to you, and my iniquity I do not hide. I confess my transgressions to you. Forgive the iniquity of my sins. You are my hiding place. Preserve me from trouble and surround me with songs of deliverance.

BIOY: 2 Chronicles 33-36 (124/241)

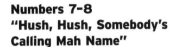

Numbers 7-8
"Hush, Hush, Somebody's Calling Mah Name"

HUSH, Hush, Somebody's callin' mah name.
Hush, Hush, Somebody's callin' mah name.
Hush, Hush, Somebody's callin' mah name.
Oh mah Lawd, Oh mah Lawdie what shall I do?

1 I'm so glad, trouble don't last always, ... (3x)
2 Sounds like Jesus, somebody's
    callin' mah name, ... (3x)
3 Soon one mornin', death'll come
    creepin' in mah room, ... (3x)
4 I'm so glad, ah got mah religion in time, ... (3x)
5 I'm so glad, I'm on mah journey home, ... (3x)
(Songs of Zion 1981, 100)

Prayer Focus: Lord, I'm listening for my name.

BIOY: Ezra 1-3 (125/240)

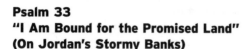

Psalm 33
"I Am Bound for the Promised Land"
(On Jordan's Stormy Banks)

I AM bound for the promised land,
I am bound for the promised land,
O who will come and go with me?
I am bound for the promised land.

1   On Jordan's stormy banks I stand,
    And cast a wishful eye,
    To Canaan's fair and happy land,
    Where my possessions lie.

2   All o'er those wide extended plains,
    Shines one eternal day;
    There God the Son for ever reigns,
    And scatters night away.

3   No chilling winds, nor pois'nous breath,
    Can reach that healthful shore,
    Sickness and sorrow, pain and death,
    Are felt and feared no more.

(Boatner and Townsend 1927, 41)

Prayer Focus: Lord, I'm on my way home!

BIOY: Ezra 4-6 (126/239)

Numbers 9-10
"I an' Satan Had a Race"

1   I AN' Satan had a race, *Hallelu, hallelu,*
     I an' Satan had a race, *Hallelu, hallelu.*
2   Win de race agin de course, ...
3   Satan tell me to my face, ...
4   He will break my kingdom down, ...
5   Jesus whisper in my heart, ...
6   He will build 'em up again, ...
7   Satan mount de iron grey; ...
8   Ride half way to Pilot-Bar, ...
9   Jesus mount de milk-white horse, ...
10   Say you cheat my fader children, ...
11   Say you cheat 'em out of glory, ...
12   Trouble like a gloomy cloud, ...
13   Gader dick an' tunder loud, ...

(Allen, Ware, and Garrison 1867, 40)

Prayer Focus: I press to the goal for the prize.

Psalm 34
"I Been in de Storm so Long"

I BEEN in de storm so long,
I been in de storm so long, chillun,
I been in de storm so long,
Oh, gimme little time to pray.

1   Oh, let me tell you, Mother,
    how I come 'long,
    Oh, gimme little time to pray,
    With a hung down head and a achin' heart,
    Oh, gimme little time to pray.

2   Now when I get to Heaven
    I'll take my seat,
    Oh, gimme little time to pray,
    An a cast my crown at my Jesus' feet,
    Oh, gimme little time to pray.

(Songs of Zion 1981, 144)

Prayer Focus: Many are the afflictions of the righteous, but you deliver us out of them all. Glory!

BIOY: Nehemiah 1-3 (128/237)

Numbers 11-12
"I Can't Stand the Fire" (Ps. 66:8-12)

I CAN'T stan' de fire, (dear sister)
I can't stan' de fire, (O Lord)
I can't stan' de fire,
While Jordan da roll so swift* (Tiddy 'Rinah).
(Allen, Ware, and Garrison 1867, 42)

* (O Lord, I) Can't stand the fire.

Prayer Focus: You, O God, have proven us. You have refined us as silver is refined. You brought us into the net. You laid affliction on our backs. You have caused others to ride over our heads. We went through fire and through water; but, you brought us out to rich fulfillment. O Lord, many are our afflictions, but we've learned that you can deliver us out of them all. You have brought us through slavery and segregation. You have preserved our spirituals and surrounded us with songs of deliverance.

BIOY: Nehemiah 4-7 (129/236)

Psalm 35
"I Can't Stay Away"

LORD, I can't stay away, I can't stay away,
I can't stay away, I can't stay away.

1 I've got to go to judgment to stand my trial,
   I've got to go to judgment to stand my trial,
   I've got to go to judgment to stand my trial,
   I can't stay away.

2 I've got to go to heav'n to live with Jesus,
   I've got to go to heav'n to live with Jesus,
   I've got to go to heav'n to live with Jesus,
   I can't stay away.

3 They're comin' from the East,
   Comin' from the West,
   Comin' from the North, Comin' from the South;
   Comin' on the rainbow, Comin' from the clouds,
   Lord, I can't stay away.

(Boatner and Townsend 1927, 57)

Prayer Focus: Plead my case, O Lord, please!

BIOY: Nehemiah 8-11 (130/235)

DAY 131

Numbers 13-14
"I Can't Stay Behind"

I CAN'T stay behind, my Lord,
I can't stay behind!

1   Dere's room enough, Room enough,
    Room enough in de heaven, my Lord;*
    Room enough, I can't stay behind.

2   I been all around, I been all around,
    Been all around de Heaven, my Lord.

3   I've searched every room—
    in de Heaven, my Lord.†

4   De angels singin'‡ — all round de trone.

5   My Fader call — call and I must go.

6   Sto-back,§ member; sto-back, member.

(Allen, Ware, and Garrison 1867, 6)

* For you.
† And Heaven all around.
‡ Crowned.
§ "Sto-back" means "Shout backwards."

Prayer Focus: I'm bound for the Promised Land!

BIOY: Nehemiah 12-13 (131/234)

Psalm 36
"I Couldn't Hear Nobody Pray"

AN' I couldn't hear nobody pray, O, Lord,
I couldn't hear nobody pray, O, Lord,
O, 'way down yonder by myself an'
I couldn't hear nobody pray,

1 In de valley, *I couldn't hear nobody pray,*
   On a my knees, *I couldn't hear nobody pray.*
   Wid my burden, *I couldn't hear nobody pray.*
   An' a my Savior, *I couldn't hear nobody pray,*
   O, Lord,

2 Chilly water, ... In a de Jordan, ...
   Crossin' over, ... In-a to Canaan, ...

3 Hallelujah, ... Troubles am over, ...
   In de Kingdom, ... Wid a my Jesus, ...

(Johnson and Johnson 1925, 89)

Prayer Focus: I'm gonna' pray, pray, pray—even when I'm way down yonder by myself!

BIOY: Esther 1-2 (132/233)

◎◎◎◎◎◎◎◎◎◎◎◎◎◎◎◎◎◎◎◎◎◎◎◎◎

Numbers 15–16
"I Don't Feel Weary"

I DON'T feel weary and noways tired,
O glory hallelujah.
1   Jest let me in the kingdom,
    While the world is all on fire.
    O glory hallelujah.
2   Gwine to live with God forever, …
3   And keep the ark a moving, …

(Allen, Ware, and Garrison 1867, 70)

Prayer Focus: Lord, I don't feel noways tired, I've come too far from where you've brought me from. The road to glory land is not easy. The going is rough, the going is tough, and the hills are hard to climb. Nevertheless, great is your faithfulness. I don't believe you brought me this far to leave me. So move me up a little higher; I want to see my Jesus!

BIOY: Esther 3–5 (133/232)

Psalm 37
"I Done Done What Ya' Tol' Me to Do"

SO glad I done done,*
So glad I done done,
So glad I done done,
I done done a-what ya' tol' me to do.
1   Tol' me to pray,
    an' I done pray,
    Tol' me to pray,
    an' I done pray.

(Johnson and Johnson 1925, 180)

* Thank God, I done done, . . . (Last ending)

Prayer Focus: "And the Lord shall help them and deliver them; He shall deliver them from the wicked, And save them, Because they trust in Him" (Ps. 37:40). If I wait on you, Lord, and keep your way, exalt me to inherit the land. In you I trust and obey.

BIOY: Esther 6-9 (134/231)

Numbers 17-18
"I Feel Like My Time Ain't Long"

I FEEL like,
I feel like, Lord,
I feel like my time ain't long;
1 Went to de graveyard de other day,
I feel like my time ain't long,
I looked at de place where my mother lay,
I feel like my time ain't long.
2 Sometimes I'm up an' sometimes I'm down, ...
An' sometimes I'm almos' on de groun', ...
3 Mind out, my brother, how you walk de cross, ...
Yo' foot might slip an' yo' soul git los', ...

(Johnson and Johnson 1926, 174)

Prayer Focus: When death come knocking at my door make death behave nice and my trip easy.

∞∞∞∞∞∞∞∞∞∞∞∞∞∞∞∞∞∞∞∞∞∞∞∞∞

Psalm 38
"I Got a Home in-a Dat Rock"

I GOT a home in a dat Rock, Don't you see?
I got a home in a dat Rock, Don't you see?
Between de earth an' sky,
    Thought I heard my Saviour cry,
you got a home in a dat Rock, Don't you see?

1   Poor man Lazrus, poor as I, Don't you see? (2x)
    Poor man Lazrus, poor as I,
    When he died he foun' a home on high,
    He had a home in a dat Rock, Don't you see?

2   Rich man, Dives, He lived so well,
        Don't you see? (2x)
    Rich man, Dives, he lived so well,
    When he died he foun' a home in Hell,
    He had no home in a dat Rock, Don't you see?

3   God gave Noah de Rainbow sign,
        Don't you see? (2x)
    God gave Noah de Rainbow sign,
    No mo water but fire nex' time,
    Better get a home in a dat Rock, Don't you see?
                        (Johnson and Johnson 1925, 96)

Prayer Focus: In you, O Lord, does my hope rest (cf. Ps. 38:15).

BIOY: Job 4-6 (136/229)

DAY 137

Numbers 19-20
"I Hear from Heaven Today"

HURRY* on, my weary soul,
And I yearde from heaven today,
Hurry on, my weary† soul,
And I yearde from heaven today.

1   My sin is forgiven and my soul set free,
    And I yearde from heaven today,
    My sin is forgiven, and my soul set free,
    And I yearde from heaven today.
2   A baby born in Bethlehem, ...
3   De trumpet sound in de oder bright land‡, ...
4   My name is called and I must go, ...
5   De bell is a ringin' in de oder bright world, ...

(Allen, Ware, and Garrison 1867, 2)

* Travel.
† My brudder, Brudder Jacob, Sister Mary
‡ World.

Prayer Focus: God bless the preacher!

Psalm 39
"I Heard de Preachin' of de Word o' God"

I HEARD de preachin' of de Elder,
Preachin' de word, preachin' de word,
I heard de preachin' of de Elder,
Preachin' de word o' God.

1 How long did it rain? Can anyone tell?
   Preachin' de word o' God,
   For forty days an' nights it fell,
   Preachin' de word o' God.

2 How long was Jonah in de belly of de whale? ...
   'Twas three whole days an' nights he sailed, ...

3 When I was a mourner
   I mourned 'til I got through, ...
   My knees got acquainted wid de hillside too, ...

(Johnson and Johnson 1926, 90)

Prayer Focus: Bless the message and messenger.

BIOY: Job 10-12 (138/227)

Numbers 21-22
"I Know de Lord's Laid His Hands on Me"

O, I KNOW de Lord, I know de Lord,
I know de Lord's laid his hands on me;
O, I know de Lord, I know de Lord,
I know de Lord's laid his hands on me.

1   Did ever you see de like befo'
    I know de Lord's laid his hands on me;
    King Jesus preachin' to de po'
    I know de Lord's laid his hands on me.

2   O, wasn't a dat a happy day, ...
    When Jesus washed my sins away, ...

3   Some seek de Lord an' don't seek right, ...
    Dey fool all day an' trifle all night, ...

4   My Lord has done jes' what He said, ...
    He's healed de sick an' raised de dead, ...

(Johnson and Johnson 1926, 164)

Prayer Focus: Thank you—my soul has been redeemed!

Psalm 40
"I Known When I'm Going Home"

OLD Satan told me to my face, O yes, Lord,
De God I seek I never find, O yes, Lord.
True believer, I know when I gwine home,
True believer, I know when I gwine home,
True believer, I know when I gwine home,
I been afraid to die.

(Allen, Ware, and Garrison 1867, 30)

Prayer Focus: Obedience is better than sacrifice (cf. Ps. 40:6–8). I love you, Lord. You heard my cry and pitied my every groan, you brought me up out of a horrible pit and miry clay and set my feet upon a rock. You established my steps and put a new song in my mouth. Many are the works you have done! Praise God! Unto you, O Lord, will I trust and obey!

BIOY: Job 16-19 (140/225)

Numbers 23–24
"I Saw the Beam in My Sister's Eye"
(Matt. 7:1-5)

1 I SAW de beam in my sister's* eye,
   Can't saw de beam in mine;
   You'd better lef ' your sister door,
   Go keep your own door clean.
2 And I had a mighty battle
       like-a Jacob and de angel,
   Jacob, time of old;
   I didn't 'tend to lef' 'em go
   Till Jesus bless my soul.

(Allen, Ware, and Garrison 1867, 17)

* Titty Peggy, Brudder Mosey, ...

Prayer Focus: Help me, Lord, to be less judgmental and hypocritical, and more understanding and compassionate. Help me to listen, gather facts, and examine my own life first, then cover my speech and actions with love.

BIOY: Job 20-22 (141/224)

Psalm 41
"I Stood on de Ribber ob Jerdon"

1   I STOOD on de ribber ob Jerdon,
    to see dat ship come sailin' ober;
    stood on de ribber ob Jerdon,
    to see dat ship sail by.
    O moaner, don' ya weep,
    when ya see dat ship come sailin' ober,
    Shout "Glory Hallelujah!"
    When ya see dat ship sail by.

2   O sister, ya bettuh be ready, …
    Brother, ya bettuh be ready, …

3   O preacher, ya bettuh be ready, …
    Deacon, ya bettuh be ready, …

(Songs of Zion 1981, 149)

Prayer Focus: Lord, I'm ready. 'Tis the Old Ship of Zion that I'm waiting for to carry me home.

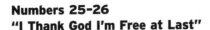

Numbers 25-26
"I Thank God I'm Free at Last"

FREE at las' — free at las'
I thank God I'm free at las'
Free at las' — free at las'
I thank God I'm free at las'.

1 Way down yonder in de grave yard walk,
  I thank God I'm free at las'
  Me an' my Jesus gwinter meet an' talk,
  I thank God I'm free at las'

2 On a my knees when de light pass by, ...
  Tho't my soul would-a rise an' fly, ...

3 Some o' dese mornin's bright an fair, ...
  Gwinter meet my Jesus, in de middle of de air, ...

(Johnson and Johnson 1926, 158)

Prayer Focus: Lord, you set me free! Glory!

BIOY: Job 27-29 (143/222)

Psalm 42
"I Want God's Heab'n to Be Mine"

YES, I want God's heab'n to be mine,
To be mine, to be mine;
Yes, I want God's heab'n to be mine,
Save me, Lord, save me.

1 I hail to my mother,
   my mother hail to me
   an' de las' word I heard her say,
   Save me Lord, save me.

2 I hail to my leader,
   my leader hail to me
   an' de las' word I heard him say,
   Save me Lord, save me.

(Johnson and Johnson 1926, 88)

Prayer Focus: My soul thirsts for you. When can I come and appear before you in heaven? There are so many people I want to meet and greet there.

BIOY: Job 30-33 (144/221)

Numbers 27-28
"Glory, Glory Hallelujah!"

1 GLORY, glory, hallejuah!
Since I laid my burden down,
Glory, glory, hallejuah!
Since I laid my burden down.

2 I feel better, so much better, …

3 Feel like shouting "Hallejuah!" …

4 Burdens down Lord, burdens down Lord, …

5 I am climbing Jacob's ladder, …

6 Ev'ry round goes higher and higher, …

7 I'm goin' home to be with Jesus, …

(Warren 1997, 38)

Prayer Focus: Lord, I cannot bear these burdens alone. I hear that you are a mighty good burden bearer and heavy load sharer. Here, Lord, I lay my burdens down before your altar and leave them in your care. I feel better, so much better!

BIOY: Job 34-35 (145/220)

Psalm 43
"You Must Be Pure and Holy"

1 WHEN I was wicked an' a prone to sin
   My Lord, brethren, ah my Lord!
   I thought that I couldn't be born again,
   My Lord, brethren, ah my Lord!
   You must be pure and holy,
   You must be pure an' a holy,
   You must be pure and holy,
   To see God feed his lambs.
2 I'll run round the cross and cry,
   My Lord, brethren, ah my Lord,
   Or give me Jesus, or I die,
   My Lord, brethren, ah my Lord!
                         (Allen, Ware, and Garrison 1867, 107)

Prayer Focus: Lord, I want to be pure and holy. Wash me, Lord Jesus, with thy hand of mercy.

BIOY: Job 36-37 (146/219)

Numbers 29-30
"I Want to Die Easy When I Die"

I WANT to die eas-y, when I die, when I die;
I want to die eas-y, when I die, when I die;
I want to die eas-y, when I die,
Shout salvation as I fly,
I want to die eas-y, when I die, when I die.

1 I want to see my mother, *when I die, when I die,*
   I want to see my mother, *when I die,*
   Shout salvation as I fly,
   I want to see my mother, *when I die, when I die.*

2 I want to see my Jesus, ...

(Johnson and Johnson 1926, 46)

Prayer Focus: Lord, take my fear of death away.

BIOY: Job 38-41 (147/218)

Psalm 44
"I Want to Die Like-a Lazarus"
(Luke 16:19-31; cf. Ps. 49:6-7)

{TITTY 'Ritta}* die like-a Lazarus die,
Die like-a Lazarus die,
I want to die like-a Lazarus die,
like-a Lazarus die, like-a Lazarus die.

(Allen, Ware, and Garrison 1867, 98)

* {I want to}

Prayer Focus: [Lazarus = One whom God helps] "A little that a righteous man has Is better than the riches of many wicked. For the arms of the wicked shall be broken, But the Lord upholds the righteous" (Ps. 37:16–17). Lord, wash me. Clean me with the blood of the Lamb. Renew my mind. Create in me a clean heart. Order my steps, forsake me not.

Numbers 31-32
"I Want to Go Home"
(Rev. 21-22)

DERE'S no rain to wet you.
O yes, I want to go home,
Want to go home.

2 Dere's no sun to burn you,—Oh yes, etc.... .
3 Dere's no hard trials, ...
4 Dere's no whips a-crackin', ...
5 Dere's no stormy weather, ...
6 Dere's no tribulation, ...
7 *No more slavery in de kingdom, ...
8 No evil-doers in de kingdom, ...
9 All is gladness in de kingdom, ...

(Allen, Ware, and Garrison 1867, 46)

* [Verse 7 was added after the Emancipation
Proclamation. – J.S.R.]

Prayer Focus: I want to enter through the gates (Rev. 22:14). Lord, help me to trust you and obey!

Psalm 45
"I Want to Join the Band"

WHAT is that up yonder I see?
Two little angels comin' a' tor me;
I want to jine the band,
I want to jine the band, (Sing together)
I want to jine the band.

(Allen, Ware, and Garrison 1867, 95)

Prayer Focus: Lord, sign me up for the Christian Jubilee. Sign my name on heaven's roll. I want a seat at the great coronation. I know there will be people coming from all nations. It'll be such a wonderful occasion when they crown you Lord of lords. Yes, I want to be in that band, in that congregation, in that holy number when they crown you King of kings. I got my invitation. I'm ready for that eternal vacation. Come on, angels, I'm down here waiting on this earthly station.

BIOY: Psalms 5–8 (150/215)

Numbers 33-34
"I Will Trust in the Lord"

1   I WILL trust in the Lord, I will trust in the Lord,
    I will trust in the Lord, till I die;
    I will trust in the Lord,
    I will trust in the Lord,
    I will trust in the Lord, till I die.

2   Sister, will you trust in the Lord, ...

3   Brother, will you trust in the Lord, ...

4   Preacher, will you trust in the Lord, ...

(The AME Zion Bicentennial Hymnal 1996, 75)

Prayer Focus: Lord, you have proven yourself to the Israelites, to the Egyptians and their gods, to enslaved African Americans, and to me. I've had my share of life's ups and downs, tears, and sorrow. I've had questions about tomorrow, but through it all, I've learned to trust, obey, and depend on your Word.

BIOY: Psalms 9-12 (151/214)

Psalm 46
"I Wish I Been Dere"

1   MY mudder, you follow Jesus,
     My sister, you follow Jesus,
     My brudder, you follow Jesus,
     To fight until I die.

2   I wish I been dere,*
     To climb Jacob's ladder,
     I wish I been dere,*
     To wear de starry crown.

(Allen, Ware, and Garrison 1867, 29)

*yonder

Prayer Focus: "Be still, and know that I am God; I will be exalted among the nations, I will be exalted in the earth" (Ps. 46:10)! Lord God, you are my refuge and my strength; a very present help in trouble. I exalt thee!

BIOY: Psalms 13-16 (152/213)

Numbers 35–36
"I'm a-Trouble in De Mind"

1   I AM a-trouble in de mind,
    O I am a-trouble in de mind;
    I ask my Lord what shall I do,
    I am a trouble in de mind.
2   I'm a trouble in de mind,
    What you doubt for?*
    I'm a trouble in de mind.

(Allen, Ware, and Garrison 1867, 30)

* Titty Rosy, Brudder Johnny, Come along dere.

Prayer Focus: Oh, my Lord, Oh, my Lord, what shall I do? What shall I do? Hush! Hush! somebody's calling my name. Run! I better run, find me a hiding place! Lord, I'm so glad, I found me a hiding place over in the Promised Land! Glory hallelujah!

BIOY: Psalms 17–19 (153/212)

Psalm 47
"I'm a-Rollin'"

I'M a rollin', I'm a rollin',
I'm a rollin' through an unfriendly worl',
I'm a rollin', I'm a rollin',
*   through an unfriendly worl';*
I'm a rollin', I'm a rollin',
I'm a rollin' through an unfriendly worl',
I'm a rollin', I'm a rollin'
*   through an unfriendly worl';*

1   O, brothers, won't you help me,
    O, brothers, won't you help me to pray;
    Oh, brothers, won't you help me,
    won't you help me in de service of de Lord.
2   O, sisters, won't you help me, ...

(Johnson and Johnson 1925, 145)

Prayer Focus: O God, King of all the earth, to you I clap my hands, shout with a triumphant voice, and sing praises with understanding. Hallelujah!

BIOY: Psalms 20-22 (154/211)

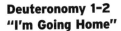
Deuteronomy 1-2
"I'm Going Home"

1   I SOUGHT my Lord in de wilderness,
    in de wilderness, in de wilderness;
    I sought my Lord in de wilderness,
    For I'm a-going home.
    For I'm going home,
    For I'm going home;
    I'm just getting ready,
    For I'm going home.

2   I found free grace in the wilderness, ...

3   My father preaches in the wilderness, ...

           (Allen, Ware, and Garrison 1867, 84)

Prayer Focus: Thank you for the courage to worship you in spirit, in truth, and in loud praises among the assembly of believers without fear of legalized persecution or the threats of an oppressor.

BIOY: Psalms 23-25 (155/210)

Psalm 48
"I'm Gonna Sing" (Acts 5:29)

1 I'M gonna sing *when the Spirit says sing,*
   I'm gonna sing *when the Spirit says sing;*
   I'm gonna sing *when the Spirit says sing,*
   And obey the Spirit of the Lord.
2 I'm gonna shout, …
3 I'm gonna preach, …
4 I'm gonna pray, …
5 I'm gonna sing, ….

(The New National Baptist Hymnal 1977, 498)

Prayer Focus: Fire, shut up in my bones, like Jeremiah, just won't leave me alone (Jer. 20:9)! I'm going to sing, shout, preach, and pray by the power of your anointing. Your Spirit is moving in me and I can't sit down! Glory! I got to tell it, on the mountain, over the hills, and everywhere that Jesus saves! Jesus saves! Jesus is the answer for the world.

BIOY: Psalms 26-29 (156/209)

Deuteronomy 3-4
"I'm Gwine Up to Heab'n Anyhow"
(Matt. 5:10-12)

ANYHOW, anyhow, anyhow my Lord!
Anyhow, yes, anyhow;
I'm gwine up to heab'n anyhow.
1   If yo' brudder talk about you,
    An' scandalize yo' name,
    Down at de cross, you mus' bow,
    I'm gwine up to heab'n anyhow.
2   If yo' sister talk about you, ...
3   If yo' preacher talk about you, ...
4   If yo' deacon talk about you, ...
               (Johnson and Johnson 1926, 126)

Prayer Focus: I've been 'buked and I've been scorned; but I heard you say, "Blessed are you when they revile and persecute you, and say all kinds of evil against you falsely for My sake" (Matt. 5:11).

Psalm 49
"I'm in Trouble"

1 I'M in trouble, Lord,
   I'm in trouble,
   I'm in trouble, Lord,
   trouble about my grave,
   trouble about my grave.
2 Sometimes I weep,
   Sometimes I mourn,
   I'm in trouble about my grave;
   Sometimes I can't do neither one,
   I'm in trouble about my grave.

(Allen, Ware, and Garrison 1867, 94)

Prayer Focus: "I sought the Lord, and He heard me, And delivered me from all my fears" (Ps. 34:4). Lord I have tasted and see that you are good; therefore I am blessed because I put my trust in you.

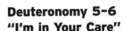

Deuteronomy 5-6
"I'm in Your Care"

OH, Lord, I'm in your care,
Oh, Lord, I'm in your care,
Ev'ry time I pray
These are the words I say,
Oh, Lord, I'm in your care.

1   Paul and Silas bound in jail, (2x)
Every time they prayed,
These are the words they said, ...

2   There was Daniel in the lion's den, ...

3   The Hebrew children in the fiery furnace, ...

(Boatner and Townsend 1927, 72)

Prayer Focus: Lord, I love you with all of my heart, with all of my soul, and with all of my might. Your words and commandments I treasure in my heart. I commit myself to you. O Lord, I'm in your care. Break me, mold me, fill me, use me in thy service.

BIOY: Psalms 36-38 (159/206)

Psalm 50
"I'm So Glad"

1   I'M so glad trouble don't last alway,
    I'm so glad trouble don't last alway,
    I'm so glad trouble don't last alway,
    Oh my Lord, Oh my Lord, what shall I do?

2   Make more room, Lord, in my heart for Thee, ...

3   I'm so glad my soul's got a hiding place, ...

4   I'm so glad I've got my religion in time, ...

5   I'm so glad the devil can do me no harm, ...

(Boatner and Townsend 1927, 17)

Prayer Focus: "Call upon Me in the day of trouble; I will deliver you, and you shall glorify Me" (Ps. 50:15). "Whoever offers praise glorifies Me; And to him who orders his conduct aright I will show the salvation of God" (Ps. 50:23). Praise be to my God and my Lord! It's me again. Help me, Lord.

BIOY: Psalms 39–42 (160/205)

Deuteronomy 7-8
"I'm Troubled in Mind"

I'M troubled, I'm troubled,
I'm troubled in mind,
If Jesus don't help me
I sho'ly will die.

1   Oh, Jesus my Saviour,
    on Thee I'll depen',
    When troubles am near me,
    You'll be my true friend.

2   When ladened wid trouble,
    an' burden'd wid grief;
    To Jesus in secret,
    I'll go for relief.

(Johnson and Johnson 1925, 120)

Prayer Focus: Lord I am hard pressed on every side, yet not crushed; perplexed, but not in despair, persecuted but not forsaken (2 Cor. 4:8–9). Thank you!

BIOY: Psalms 43-45 (161/204)

Psalm 51
"I've Been 'Buked"

1 I'VE been 'buked an' I've been scorned,
   I've been 'buked an' I've been scorned, children.
   I've been 'buked an' I've been scorned,
   I've been talked about sho's you' born.
2 Dere is trouble all over dis worl',
   Dere is trouble all over dis worl', children.
   Dere is trouble all over dis worl',
   Dere is trouble all over dis worl'.
3 Ain' gwine lay my 'ligion down,
   Ain' gwine lay my 'ligion down, children.
   Ain' gwine lay my 'ligion down,
   Ain' gwine lay my 'ligion down.

(Songs of Zion 1981, 143)

Prayer Focus: Lord, I may be struck down, but never destroyed, because you live in me. I will not lose heart; for the light affliction I experience does not compare to the atrocious realities of Calvary or slavery. I look not at things as they are, but as they will be. I will walk by faith and hold to your unchanging hand.

BIOY: Psalms 46-48 (162/203)

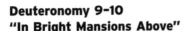

Deuteronomy 9-10
"In Bright Mansions Above"

IN bright mansions above,
In bright mansions above, Lord,
I want to live up yonder,
In bright mansions above.

1   My mother's gone to glory,
    I want to go there too, Lord,
    I want to live up yonder,
    In bright mansions above.

2   My father's gone to glory, ...
3   My brother's gone to glory, ...
4   My sister's gone to glory, ...
5   The Christian's gone to glory, ...
6   My Savior's gone to glory, ...

(Boatner and Townsend 1927, 58)

Prayer Focus: I desire more spiritual power. Along with my Bible study, help me to fast and pray.

BIOY: Psalms 49-51 (163/202)

Psalm 52
"In Dat Great Day"

OH, whah you run-nin', sinner?
I'se a run-nin' from de fi-ah,
I'se a run-nin' from de fi-ah,
In dat great day. O Isarel! O Isarel!
O Isarel! In dat great day.

1   Don' you hear you Saviour callin'?
    Don' you hear you Saviour callin'?
    Don' you hear you Saviour callin'?
    In dat Great day?

2   Don' you see de dead arisin'? …

3   Don' you heah de trumpet soundin'? …

4   Don' you see dem tombs a-bustin'? …

5   Yes, we'll see our chillen risin' …

6   Don' you see de chariot comin'? …

7   Don' you see de sinnah tremblin'? …

8   Don' you heah de saints a-shoutin'? …

(Southern 1997, 198)

Prayer Focus: I am like a green olive tree in thy house, O God. I forever trust your mercy (Ps.52:8).

BIOY: Psalms 52-55 (164/201)

Deuteronomy 11-12
"In Dat Great Gittin' Up Mornin'"

I'M a goin' to tell you 'bout
    de comin' of de Saviour,
Fare you well, Fare you well.

1   Dere's a better day a comin', FYW, FYW;*
Oh, preacher, fol' yo' bible, FYW, FYW
In dat great gittin' up mornin', FYW, FYW;
In dat great gittin' up mornin', FYW, FYW.
De Lord spoke to Gabriel, FYW, FYW;
Go look behin' de altar, FYW, FYW.
Take down de silvah trumpet, FYW, FYW.
Blow yo' trumpet Gabriel; FYW, FYW.
Den you'll see po' sinners risin', FYW, FYW;
Den you'll see de worl' on fiah, FYW, FYW.
Hear de rumblin' of de thunder, FYW, FYW.
Earth shall reel an' totter, FYW, FYW.

(Johnson and Johnson 1926, 40)

* Fare you well, Fare you well.

Prayer Focus: In that great getting-up morning, a better day and brighter tomorrow is coming.

BIOY: Psalms 56-58 (165/200)

Psalm 53
"In My Father's House" (John 14:2)

1 I'M on my way up there, *To my Father's house,*
To my Father's house, To my Father's house,
I'm on my way up there, *To my Father's house,*
There is peace, sweet peace.
2 Oh, come and go with me, …
3 I've got a mother up there, …
4 I've got a sister up there, …
5 I've got a brother up there, …
6 I've got a father up there, …

(Boatner and Townsend 1927, 62)

Prayer Focus: Eye has not seen nor ear heard the riches that my Lord has prepared for me in my Creator's house (cf. 1 Cor. 2:9). Lord, I'm grateful! Glory be to God!

BIOY: Psalms 59–61 (166/199)

Deuteronomy 13-14
"In the Mansions Above"

GOOD Lord, in de manshans above,
Good Lord, in de manshans above,
My Lord, I hope to meet
  my Jesus In de manshans above.

1   If you get to heaven before I do,
    Lord, tell my Jesus I'm a comin' too,
    To de manshans above.

2   My Lord, I've had many crosses
        an' trials here below;
    My Lord, I hope to meet you
    In de manshans above.

3   Fight on, my brudder, for de manshans above,
    For I hope to meet my Jesus dere
    In de manshans above.

(Allen, Ware, and Garrison 1867, 59)

Prayer Focus: Thank you for a home I can call my own
and a family that won't be taken from me!

BIOY: Psalms 62-64 (167/198)

Psalm 54
"In the River of Jordan" (Mark 1:4-5)

1   IN the river of Jordan John baptized,
How I longed to be baptized;
In the river of Jordan John baptized,
To the dying Lamb.
Pray on, pray on,
Pray on, my Father's children;
Pray on, pray on,
Unto the dying Lamb.

2   O we baptize all that come by faith, ...

3   Here's another one come to be baptized, ...

(Boatner and Townsend 1927, 82)

Prayer Focus: In my mind and spirit I have been buried with you through baptism into death. I've risen in a newness of life empowered by your indwelling Spirit. You died that I may live. I have died that you may live in me. My life is yours.

BIOY: Psalms 65-68 (168/197)

Deuteronomy 15-16
"It's Me, O, Lord"

IT'S me, it's me, it's me, O Lord,
Standin' in the need of prayer,
It's me, it's me, it's me, O Lord,
Standin' in the need of prayer.

1   Tain't my mother or my father,
    but it's me O, Lord,
    Standin' in the need of prayer,
    Tain't my mother or my father,
    but it's me O, Lord,
    Standin' in the need of prayer.

2   Tain't the deacon or my leader, ...

(Johnson and Johnson 1925, 94)

Prayer Focus: Lord, it's me again, standing in the need of prayer. Please, Sir Jesus, have mercy!

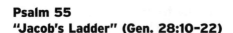

Psalm 55
"Jacob's Ladder" (Gen. 28:10-22)

I WANT to climb up Jacob's ladder,
Jacob's ladder, O Jacob's ladder,
I want to climb up Jacob's ladder,
But I can't climb it
till I make my peace with the Lord.

1   O praise ye the Lord,
    I'll praise Him till I die,
    I'll praise Him till I die,
    And sing Jerusalem.

2   O praise the Lord,
    O praise ye the Lord, ...

(Allen, Ware, and Garrison 1867, 96)

Prayer Focus: Jesus is the stairway to heaven! Lord God, I was wrong. I am sorry; please forgive me. I love you. Lord God, all to Jesus I surrender.

BIOY: Psalms 72-74 (170/195)

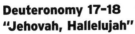
Deuteronomy 17-18
"Jehovah, Hallelujah"
(Gen. 22:1-14; Matt. 8:20)

JEHOVAH, Hallelujah,
De Lord is per-wide,*
Jehoviah, Hallelujah,
De Lord is per-wide.
De foxes have hole,
an' de birdies have a nest,
De Son of Man he dunno†
where to lay de weary head.

(Allen, Ware, and Garrison 1867, 2)

* Will provide
† Hanno (has no)

Prayer Focus: Lord, you are my Shepherd. You provide me with all of my needs. Soon I will live with you in our heavenly mansion on high! Hallelujah!

BIOY: Psalms 75-77 (171/194)

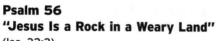
Psalm 56
"Jesus Is a Rock in a Weary Land"
(Isa. 32:2)

OH, Jesus is a rock in a weary land,
A weary land, a weary land,
Oh, Jesus is a rock in a weary land,
A shelter in the time of storm.

1 'Postle *Paul* declared Jesus is a rock in a
   'Postle *Paul* declared,
   'Postle *Paul* declared,
   'Postle *Paul* declared
   Jesus is a rock in a weary land,
   A shelter in the time of storm.

2 'Postle *John* declared, ...

(Boatner and Townsend 1927, 59)

Prayer Focus: Lord, you are my Rock, my Fortress, and my Deliverer! You are my Bridge over troubled water, the Lily of the Valley, the Rose of Sharon, the Bright and Morning Star; my Sweet Honey in a rock!

BIOY: Psalms 78–81 (172/193)

Deuteronomy 19-20
"Jesus on the Water-side"

1 HEAVEN bell a-ring, I know de road,
   Heaven bell a-ring, I know de road;
   Heaven bell a-ring, I know de road,
   Jesus sittin' on de water-side.

2 Do come along, do let us go,
   Do come along, do let us go,
   Do come along, do let us go,
   Jesus sittin' on de water-side.

(Allen, Ware, and Garrison 1867, 28)

Prayer Focus: Jesus, I've got my ticket. I'll meet you down by the riverside. I'm ready to board the Old Ship of Zion and set sail for Canaan's fair and happy land to study war no more.

BIOY: Psalms 82-84 (173/192)

Psalm 57
"Jesus, Won't You Come By-and-By?"

YOU ride dat horse,
you call him Macadoni,
Jesus, won't you come bumby?
You ride him in de mornin'
and you ride him in de evenin',
Jesus, won't you come bumby?
De Lord knows
de world's gwine to end up,
Jesus, won't you come bumby?

(Allen, Ware, and Garrison 1867, 60)

Prayer Focus: Lord, I am tossed and driven on this restless sea of time. My days are filled with swift transition. I find myself destitute of time, money, and the things that life demands. I'm drowning in sorrow. I'm consumed with despair. I need the light from heaven's lighthouse to shine on me. I know you're coming and you'll be on time.

BIOY: Psalms 85–87 (174/191)

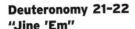

Deuteronomy 21-22
"Jine 'Em"

ON Sunday mornin' I seek my Lord;
Jine 'em, jine 'em oh!
Oh jine 'em, believer,
jine 'em so;
Jine 'em, jine 'em oh!
(Also)
Join, brethren, join us O,
Join us, join us O,
We meet tonight to sing and pray;
In Jesus' name we'll sing and pray.

(Allen, Ware, and Garrison 1867, 21)

Prayer Focus: Lord, I am glad when they say unto me: "Let's go to worship service and lift up the name of Jesus " (cf. Ps. 122:1). From the rising of the sun to its going down, your name is to be praised!

Psalm 58
"John Saw the Holy Number"
(Rev. 14:1)

JOHN saw, Oh, John saw,
John saw the holy number
sitting on the golden altar.

1   Worthy, worthy is the Lamb,
    is the Lamb, is the Lamb,
    Oh, Worthy worthy is the Lamb,
    Sitting on the golden altar.

2   Oh, Mary wept, an' Martha cried,
    Martha cried, Martha cried,
    Oh, Weeping Mary weeps no more,
    Sitting on the golden altar.

                    (Johnson and Johnson 1925, 158)

Prayer Focus: Lord, I want to see that number. I want to be in that number! God, give me a song that the angels cannot sing. I've been washed in the blood of the crucified One. I've been redeemed!

BIOY: Psalms 91–94 (176/189)

🔹🔹🔹🔹🔹🔹🔹🔹🔹🔹🔹🔹🔹🔹🔹🔹🔹🔹🔹🔹🔹🔹

Deuteronomy 23-24
"John, John, of the Holy Order"

JOHN, John, wid de holy order,*
Sittin' on de golden order;
John, John, wid de holy order,
    Sittin' on de golden order;
John, John, wid de holy order,
Sittin' on de golden order,
    To view de promised land.
O Lord, I weep, I mourn,
Why don't you move so slow?
I'm a huntin' for some guardian angel
    Gone along before.
Mary and Marta, feed my lamb,**
feed my lamb, feed my lamb;
Simon Peter, feed my lamb,
    a sittin' on de golden order.
(Allen, Ware, and Garrison 1867, 16)

  * John, John, de holy Baptist
** Paul and Silas, bound in jail

Prayer Focus: Lord, I'll move at your command. I'm listening.

BIOY: Psalms 95-97 (177/188)

Psalm 59
"Join the Angel Band"

1 IF you look up de road you see fader Mosey,
   Join de angel band,
   If you look up de road you see fader Mosey,
   Join de angel band.
2 Do, fader Mosey, gader your army, ...
3 O do mo' soul gader togeder, ...
4 O do join 'em, join 'em for Jesus, ...
5 O do join 'em, join 'em archangel, ...

(Allen, Ware, and Garrison 1867, 39)

Prayer Focus: Hear my prayer, O God. Give ear to the words of my mouth. Strangers have risen up against me and oppressors have sought after my life (Ps. 54:2–3). To you will I sing praises; for you are my defense, my strength, and my refuge in trouble.

BIOY: Psalms 98-100 (178/187)

Deuteronomy 25–26
"Jerdan's Mills"

1 JERDAN'S mills a-grinding,
  Jerdan's a-hay;
  Jerdan's mills a-grinding,
  Jerdan's a-hay.
2 Built without nail or hammer, ...
3 Runs without wind or water, ...

  (Allen, Ware, and Garrison 1867, 68)

Prayer Focus: Be merciful to me, O God, send forth your mercy and truth. My soul trusts in you. In the shadow of your wings I will make my refuge (Ps. 57:1). I cry out to you, God Most High; put my tears into your bottle (Ps. 56:8). With a mighty and outstretched arm, with great terror and with signs and wonders, turn back those who have mistreated me, afflicted me, laid hard bondage on me; those who would swallow me up. Deliver me. Songs of praises I will ever give to you (Ps. 56:12)!

BIOY: Psalms 101–103 (179/186)

Psalm 60
"Joshua Fit de Battle ob Jerico"
(Josh. 6:1-26)

JOSHUA fit de battle ob Jerico, Jerico, Jerico,
Joshua fit de battle ob Jerico,
An' de walls come tumblin' down.
You may talk about yo' king ob Gideon,
You may talk about yo' man ob Saul,
Dere's none like good ole Joshua
At de battle ob Jerico
Up to de walls ob Jerico.
He marched with spear in han'
"Go blow dem ram horns" Joshua cried,
"Kase de battle am in my han'."
Den de lam' ram sheephorns begin to blow,
     trumpets begin to soun',
Joshua commanded de chillen to shout,
An' de walls come tumblin' down
Dat morning …

(Johnson and Johnson 1925, 56)

Prayer Focus: Lord, I'll let you fight my battles!

Deuteronomy 27-28
"Jubalee"

JUBALEE, Jubalee,
O, my Lord!
Jubalee, Jubalee,
O, my Lord! Jubalee.

1   What is de matter wid de mourners,
    O, my Lord!
    De devil's in de Amen corner,
    O, Lord! Jubalee.
2   What is de matter wid ol' Zion,
    O, my Lord!
    You better stop yo' foolin' sinner man,
    O, Lord! Jubalee.

(Johnson and Johnson 1926, 142)

Prayer Focus: Lord, if I trust you and obey, I can stand on your promises. I promise to love you, my neighbor, and myself! In thee do I trust.

BIOY: Psalms 108-110 (181/184)

Psalm 61
"Just Now"

1   SANCTOFY me, sanctofy me,
    Sanctofy me, sanctofy me,
    Sanctofy me, just now;
    Just now; just now;
    Sanctofy me just now.
2   Good religion, good religion, …
3   Come to Jesus, come to Jesus, …

(Allen, Ware, and Garrison 1867, 67)

Prayer Focus: Deliver me from my enemies, O my God. Defend me from those who rise up against me. The mighty gather against me. Awaken and help me! They growl like dogs, they belch out swords and spears of iniquity. But I will sing of your power. Yes, I will sing aloud of your mercy; for you have been my defense and refuge (Ps. 59), my shelter and strong tower in a time of trouble (Ps. 61:3).

BIOY: Psalms 111-114 (182/183)

Deuteronomy 29–30
"Keep a-Inchin' Along"

KEEP a inchin' along, Keep a inchin' along,
Massa Jesus is comin' bye an' bye,
Keep a inchin' along like a po' inch worm,
Massa Jesus is comin' bye an' bye.
O Christians Keep a-inchin' along,
Keep a inchin' along,
*   Massa Jesus is comin' bye an' bye.*

1   O, I died one time gwinter die no mo'
   Massa Jesus is comin' bye an' bye.
   O, I died one time gwinter die no mo'
   Massa Jesus is comin' bye an' bye.
2   O, you in de Lord and de Lord in you, …
3   How can I die when I'm in de Lord? …

(Johnson and Johnson 1925, 134)

Prayer Focus: Lord, because you live in me and I live for you, I have hope. Therefore, I'll keep pressing on the upward way, praying as I onward go. Lord, guide my feet to holy ground.

BIOY: Psalms 115–118 (183/182)

Psalm 62
"Keep Me F'om Sinkin' Down"

OH, Lord, Oh, my Lord!
Oh, my good Lord!
Keep me f'om sinkin' down.
Oh, Lord, Oh, my Lord!
Oh, my good Lord!
Keep me f'om sinkin' down.

1   I tell you what I mean to do;
     Keep me f'om sinkin' down:
     I mean to go to heav'n too,
     Keep me f'om sinkin' down.

2   I look up yondah an' what do I see; ...
     I see de angels beckonin' me, ...

(Johnson and Johnson 1925, 154)

Prayer Focus: I'm swimming in an ocean of sin. Master, the tempest is raging. Help! Throw out the lifeline! Jesus, be ye lifted up; draw me to you.

BIOY: Psalm 119 (184/181)

Deuteronomy 31-32
"King Emanuel"

1   O MY King Emanuel, my Emanuel above,
Sing glory to my King Emanuel.

2   If you walk de golden street,
and you join de golden band,
Sing glory be to my King Emanuel.

3   If you touch one string,
den de whole heaven ring....

4   O the great cherubim,
O de cherubim above, ...

5   O believer, ain't you glad
dat your soul is converted? ...

(Allen, Ware, and Garrison 1867, 26)

Prayer Focus: Glory to your name! I shall be strong and of good courage. I shall not be afraid, for you, O Lord, go before me. You will not leave me nor forsake me. My heart sings, "Glory to your name!"

BIOY: Psalms 120-123 (185/180)

Psalm 63
"King Jesus Is a-Listenin'"

KING Jesus is a-listenin' all day long,
King Jesus is a-listenin' all day long,
King Jesus is a-listenin' all day long,
To hear some sinner pray.

1   Some say that John the Baptist
    Was nothin' but a Jew,
    But the Holy Bible tells us
    That John was a preacher too.

2   That Gospel train is comin',
    A-rumblin' through the lan',
    But I hear them wheels a-hummin',
    Get ready to board that train!

3   I know I been converted,
    I ain't gon' make no alarm,
    For my soul is bound for Glory,
    And the devil can't do me no harm.

(Songs of Zion 1981, 152)

Prayer Focus: My soul thirsts for you.

BIOY: Psalms 124-126 (186/179)

Joshua 1-2
"Kum Ba Yah"

1 KUM ba yah, my Lord, Kum ba yah!
  Kum ba yah, my Lord, Kum ba yah!
  Kum ba yah, my Lord, Kum ba yah!
  O Lord, Kum ba yah!
2 Someone's crying, Lord, Kum ba yah!
  Someone's crying, Lord, Kum ba yah!
  Someone's crying, Lord, Kum ba yah!
  O Lord, Kum ba yah!
3 Someone's singing, Lord, Kum ba yah! (3x)
  O Lord, Kum ba yah!
4 Someone's praying, Lord, Kum ba yah! (3x)
  O Lord, Kum ba yah!

(The New National Baptist Hymnal 1977, 506)

Prayer Focus: Come by here, my Lord, come by here!
Pass me not gentle Savior; hear my humble cry!

Psalm 64
"Lay This Body Down"

1   O GRAVEYARD, O graveyard,
     I'm walkin' troo de graveyard;
     Lay dis body down.
2   *I know moonlight,
     I know starlight,
     I'm walkin' troo de starlight;
     Lay dis body down.

(Allen, Ware, and Garrison 1867, 19)

   *   O moonlight (or moonrise);
       O my soul, O your soul.

Prayer Focus: Hear my voice, O God, in my meditation. Preserve my life from fear of the final enemy,
death. O death, where is your victory? Thank you for
victory over sin, hell, and the grave through Christ (1
Cor. 15:51–57).

BIOY: Psalms 130-133 (188/177)

Joshua 3-4
"Lean on the Lord's Side"

1 WAI', poor Daniel,
  He lean on de Lord's side;
  (Say) Daniel rock de lion joy,*
  Lean on de Lord's side.
2 (Say) De golden chain†
  to ease him down, ...
3 De silver spade to dig his grave, ...
                    (Allen, Ware, and Garrison 1867, 100)

  * i.e. Daniel (as if Samson) racked the lion's jaw.
  † Band.

Prayer Focus: You walked with my foreparents, Lord, now walk with me. You strengthened them, now strengthen me. You kept them, now keep me. Glory!

Psalm 65
"Let God's Saints Come In"

COME down, angel, and trouble the water,
Come down, angel, and trouble the water,
Come down, angel, and trouble the water,
And let God's saints come in. (God say you must)

1   Canaan land is the land for me,
    And let God's saints come in. (repeat)

2   There was a wicked man,
    He kept them children in Egypt land. (repeat)

3   God did say to Moses one day,
    Say Moses go to Egypt land. (repeat)

4   And tell him to let my people go,
    And Pharaoh would not let 'em go. (repeat)

5   God did go to Moses' house,
    And God did tell him who he was. (repeat)

6   God and Moses walked and talked,
    And God did show him who he was. (repeat)

(Allen, Ware, and Garrison 1867, 76)

Prayer Focus: Guide me, O thou great Jehovah!

BIOY: Psalms 137–139 (190/175)

Joshua 5-6
"Let Me Ride"

1 I'M a soldier, *let me ride,*
  I'm a soldier, *let me ride*
  I'm a soldier, *let me ride,*
  Low down your chariot, *let me ride.*
2 Been converted, let me ride, …
3 Got my ticket, let me ride, …
4 Troubles over, let me ride, …
5 In the kingdom, let me ride, …

(Boatner and Townsend 1927, 26)

Prayer Focus: Ride on King Jesus! Let me ride. I cast my lot with you. Your fight is my fight. Your victory is my victory. Where you now are, I shall be!

Psalm 66
"Let the Words" (Ps. 19:14)

LET the words of my mouth,
And the meditation of my heart
Be acceptable in Thy sight,
O Lord, my strength,
And my Redeemer,
Amen.

(Boatner and Townsend 1927, 14)

Prayer Focus: "I will praise You, O Lord, among the peoples; I will sing to You among the nations. For Your mercy reaches unto the heavens, And Your truth unto the clouds. Be exalted, O God, above the heavens; Let Your glory be above all the earth" (Ps. 57:9–11). I bless you, O God, and I will make the voice of your praise to be heard. You keep my soul among the living and you do not allow my feet to be moved. You have proven me. You bring me through fires to rich fulfillment (Ps. Glory!

Joshua 7-8
"Let Us Break Bread Together"

1   LET us break bread together on our knees,
     Let us break bread together on our knees;
     When I fall on my knees,
          With my face to the rising sun,
     O Lord, have mercy on me.

2   Let us drink the cup together on our knees,
     Let us drink the cup together on our knees;
     When I fall on my knees,
          With my face to the rising sun,
     O Lord, have mercy on me.

3   Let us praise God together on our knees,
     Let us praise God together on our knees;
     When I fall on my knees,
          With my face to the rising sun,
     O Lord, have mercy on me.

(The New National Baptist Hymnal 1977, 488)

Prayer Focus: O Lord, I have been angry, bitter, and selfish. Have mercy on my iniquity. Help me to love my neighbor.

BIOY: Psalms 147-150 (193/172)

Psalm 67
"Lis'en to de Lam's"

LIS'EN to de lam's, all a cryin'.
Lis'en to de lam's, all a cryin'.
Lis'en to de lam's, all a cryin'.
I wan'ta go to heaben when I die.

1   Come on sister wid yo' ups an' downs,
    Wan'ta go to heaben when I die.
    De angel's waitin' for to give you a crown,
    wan'ta go to heaben when I die.

2   Come on mourner an'-a don't be shame, ...
    De angel's waitin' for to write-a yo' name, ...

3   Mind out brother how you walk de cross, ...
    Yo' foot might slip a an' yo' soul get-a los', ...

                            (Johnson and Johnson 1925, 78)

Prayer Focus: "God be merciful to us and bless us, And cause His face to shine upon us" (Ps. 67:1). The blood of ancestral slaves, like sacrificial lambs, cries out for healing and restoration. Make it so, Lord.

BIOY: Proverbs 1–3 (194/171)

Joshua 9-10
"Lit'le David Play on Yo' Harp"
(1 Sam. 16:16-23; 17:1-54)

LIT'LE David play on yo' harp,
Hallelu, hallelu,
Lit'le David play on yo' harp, hallelu,
Lit'le David play on yo' harp,
Hallelu, hallelu,
Lit'le David play on yo' harp, Hallelu,
(final = Hallelu, hallelujah.)

1   Lit'le David was a shepherd boy,
    he kill'd Golia an' shout fo' joy.
    Lit'le David was a shepherd boy,
    he kill'd Golia an' shout fo' joy.

2   Joshua was de son of Nun,
    He never would quit 'till his work was done.
    Joshua was de son of Nun,
    He never would quit 'till his work was done.

(Johnson and Johnson 1925, 65)

Prayer Focus: Spirit, come upon me like David.

BIOY: Proverbs 4-6 (195/170)

Psalm 68
"Little Children, Then Won't You Be Glad?"

1 LITTLE children, then won't you be glad,
   Little children, then won't you be glad,
   That you have been to heav'n,
   an' you're gwine to go again,
   For to try on the long white robe, children,
   For to try on the long white robe.

2 King Jesus, he was so strong (ter), my Lord,
   That he jarred down the walls of hell.

3 Don't you hear what de chariot say? (bis)
   De fore wheels run by de grace ob God,
   An' de hind wheels dey run by faith.

4 Don't you 'member what you promise
       de Lord? (bis)
   You promise de Lord
   that you would feed his sheep,
   An' gather his lambs so well.

(Allen, Ware, and Garrison 1867, 87)

Prayer Focus: Blessed be the Lord who daily loads us with benefits. Give me strength this day.

BIOY: Proverbs 7–9 (196/169)

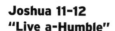

Joshua 11-12
"Live a-Humble"

LIVE a humble, humble,
Humble yourselves, the bell's done rung,
Glory and honor! Praise King Jesus!
Glory and honor, Praise the Lord!

1 Watch that sun, how steady it runs,
  Don't let it catch you with your work undone.

2 Ever see such a man as God?
  He gave up His Son for to come and die
  Gave up His Son for to come and die,
  Just to save my soul from a burning fire.

(Songs of Zion 1981, 108)

Prayer Focus: Glory and honor to you, my Lord! Help me to be humble, holy, meek, and lowly.

Psalm 69
"Look Away Into Heaven"

O LOOK away (O look away) Into heaven,
O look away (O look away) Into heaven,
O look away (O look away) Into heaven, (Lord,)
And I hope I'll join the band.

1 Goin' to see my mother, *One of these mornings,*
   Goin' to see my mother, *One of these mornings,*
   Goin' to see my mother, *One of these mornings,*
   And I hope I'll join the band.

2 Goin' to ride up in the chariot, ...
3 Goin' to meet my sister, ...
4 Goin' to meet my brother, ...
5 Goin' to meet my father, ...
6 Goin' to meet King Jesus, ...

(Boatner and Townsend 1927, 65)

Prayer Focus: Lord, keep my eyes on the prize!

BIOY: Proverbs 13-15 (198/167)

Joshua 13-14
"Look-a How Dey Done My Lord"

1   LOOK-A how dey done my Lord, (4x)
     done my Lord, done my Lord, (2x)
     He never said a mumblin' word, (4x)
     not a word, not a word, (2x)

2   Dey saw him when he rise an' fall, (4x)
     rise an' fall, rise an' fall, (2x)
     Dey carry him to Calvary, (4x)
     Calvary, Calvary, (2x)

3   He had to wear a thorny crown, (4x)
     thorny crown, thorny crown, (2x)
     Dey carry him to Pilate's Hall, (4x)
     Pilate's Hall, Pilate's Hall, (2x)

4   Dey licked him wid violence, (4x)
     violence, violence, (2x)
     An' den dey nailed him to de tree, (4x)
     to de tree, to de tree, (2x)

(Johnson and Johnson 1926, 168)

Prayer Focus: On a tree you died for me. Mercy!

BIOY: Proverbs 16-18 (199/166)

Psalm 70
"Lord, I Want to Be a Christian in-a My Heart"

1   LORD, I want to be a Christian
in-a my heart, in-a my heart,
Lord, I want to be a Christian, in-a my heart.

2   I don't want to be like Judas …
I don't want to be like Judas in-a my heart.

3   Lord I want to be more holy, …
Lord I want to be more holy in-a my heart.

4   I just want to be like Jesus …
I just want to be like Jesus in-a my heart.

(Johnson and Johnson 1926, 72)

Prayer Focus: Lord, I want to be a Christian in my heart. With my whole heart, I want to love you, honor you, obey you, and do your will. I want to love everybody.

BIOY: Proverbs 19-22 (200/165)

Joshua 15–16
"Lord, Make Me More Patient"

LORD, make me more patient,*
Lord, make me more patient,
Lord, make me more patient,
Until we meet again;
Patient, patient, patient,
Until we meet again.

(Allen, Ware, and Garrison 1867, 52)

* "Any adjective expressive of the virtues is inserted
here: holy, loving, peaceful, etc."

Prayer Focus: Lord, you say count it all joy when I fall
into various trials, knowing that the testing of my faith
produces patience that I may be mature and complete,
lacking nothing (James 1:2–4). Father, I stretch my
hand to thee; no other help I know. Guard my heart
and mind with peace that none other has ever known
through Christ Jesus (Phil. 4:6–7).

Psalm 71
"Lord, Remember Me"

1   OH Deat' he is a little man,
    And he goes from do' to do',
    He kill some souls and he wounded some,
    And he lef ' some souls to pray.
    Oh* Lord, remember me,
    Do, Lord, remember me;
    Remember me† as de year roll round,
    Lord, remember me.

2   I want to die like-a Jesus die,
    And he die wid a free good will,
    I lay out in de grave and I stretchee out e arms,
    Do, Lord, remember me.

                    (Allen, Ware, and Garrison 1867, 12)

* Do.
† I pray (cry) to de Lord.

Prayer Focus: Remember me, remember me, O Lord, remember me. Omnipotent One, I stretch my hand to thee.

BIOY: Proverbs 26-28 (202/163)

Joshua 17-18
"Mah God Is So High"
(John 10:9; cf. 14:6)

MAH God is so high, yuh can't get over Him;
He's so low, yuh can't git under Him;
He's so wide, yuh can't get aroun' Him;
Yuh mus' come in by an through de Lam'.

1   One day as I was a-walkin'
    along de Hebenly road,
    Mah Savior spoke unto me,
    an' He fill mah heart wid His love.

2   I'll take mah gospel trumpet
    an' I'll begin to blow,
    An' if mah Savior help me,
    I'll blow wherever I go.

(Songs of Zion 1981, 105)

Prayer Focus: Someone's knocking at the door; someone's ringing the bell. Open up, Lord, let me in!

BIOY: Proverbs 29-31 (203/162)

Psalm 72
"Many Thousand Go"

1   NO more peck o' corn for me,
    No more, no more;
    No more peck o' corn for me,
    Many tousand go.
2   No more driver's lash for me, ...
3   No more pint o' salt for me, ...
4   No more hundred lash for me, ...
5   No more mistress' call for me, ...
    (Allen, Ware, and Garrison 1867, 48)

[**NOTE:** A song "to which the Rebellion had actually given rise. This was composed by nobody knows whom—though it was the most recent doubtless of all these 'spirituals,'—and had been sung in secret to avoid detection. It is certainly plaintive enough. The peck of corn and pint of salt were slavery's rations."—T.W.H. Lt. Col. Trowbridge learned that it was first sung when Beauregard took the slaves of the islands to build the fortifications at Hilton Head and Bay Point.]

Prayer Focus: Blessed be the name of the Lord!

BIOY: Ecclesiastes 1-4 (204/161)

Joshua 19–20
"Mary an' Martha Jes' Gone 'Long"

1 MARY an' Martha jes' gone 'long,
   Mary an' Martha jes' gone 'long,
   Mary an' Martha jes' gone 'long,
   To ring dem charmin' bells, (O, Yes, Sister)

2 Cryin', Free grace an' dyin' love,
   Free grace an' dyin' love,
   Free grace an' dyin' love,
   To ring dem charmin' bells.

3 O, de preacher an' elder jes' gone 'long, (3x)
   To ring dem charmin' bells.

4 My ol' mother an' father jes' gone 'long, (3x)
   To ring dem charmin' bells.

5 O, 'way over Jordan, Lord, (3x)
   To ring dem charmin' bells.

(Johnson and Johnson 1926, 81)

Prayer Focus: Plead our case, Lord, before God's uncompromising throne. May his grace and mercy shine all around us.

BIOY: Ecclesiastes 5–6 (205/160)

Psalm 73
"Mary Had a Baby, Yes, Lord"

1 MARY had a baby, Yes Lord!
  Mary had a baby, Yes, my Lord;
  Mary had a baby, Yes, Lord!
  De people keep-a comin' an' de train done gone.
2 What did she name Him? Yes, Lord! (3x)
  De people keep-a comin' an' de train done gone.
3 She name him King Jesus, Yes, Lord! (3x)
  De people keep-a comin' an' de train done gone.
4 She name him Mighty Couns'lor, Yes, Lord!(3x)
  De people keep-a comin' an' de train done gone.
5 Oh, where was he born? Yes, Lord! (3x)
  De people keep-a comin' an' de train done gone.
6 Oh, born in a manger, Yes, Lord! (3x)
  De people keep-a comin' an' de train done gone.

(Johnson and Johnson 1926, 124)

Prayer Focus: Like the underground railroad, Lord, deliver many a thousand on the morning train.

BIOY: Ecclesiastes 7-9 (206/159)

Joshua 21-22
"Meet, O Lord"
(Rev. 19:11; 21:6-7)

1   MEET, O Lord, on de milk-white horse,
   An' de nineteen wile* in his han';
   Drop on, drop on de crown on my head,
   An' rolly in my Jesus' arm.
   In dat mornin' all day,
   In dat mornin' all day,
   In dat mornin' all day,
   When Jesus de Chris' been born.

2   Moon went into de poplar tree,
   An' star went into blood;
   In dat mornin', etc.

(Allen, Ware, Garrison 1867, 43)

* i.e. the anointing vial.

Prayer Focus: King Jesus, crown your saints with the fruit of your Spirit (Gal. 5:22–23). Amen.

BIOY: Ecclesiastes 10-12 (207/158)

Psalm 74
"Members, Don't Git Weary"
(Gal. 6:9-10)

MEMBERS, don't git weary,
*   Members, don't git weary,*
Members, don't git weary,
*   for de work's mos' done.*

1   O, keep yo' lamp trim'd an' a-burnin', (3x)
    for de work's mos' done.

2   I'm gwine down to de ribbuh ob Jordan,
    O Yes, gwine down to de ribbuh ob Jordan (2x)
    When my work is done.

3   I'm gwine set at de welcome table,
    O Yes , gwine set at de welcome table (2x)
    When my work is done.

4   I'm gwine feas' on de milk an' honey,
    O Yes, feas' on de milk an' honey (2x)
    When my work is done.

5   I'm gwinter march wid de talles' angel,
    O Yes, march wid de talles' angel (2x)
    When my work is done.

(Johnson and Johnson 1926, 155)

Prayer Focus: Lord, I want to see what the end will be. I want to sit at the welcome table and feast on milk and honey.

BIOY: Song of Solomon 1-4 (208/157)

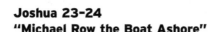

Joshua 23-24
"Michael Row the Boat Ashore"

1. MICHAEL Row de boat ashore, Hallelujah!
2. Michael boat a gospel boat, Hallelujah!
3. I wonder where my mudder deh (there), Hallelujah!
4. See my mudder on de rock gwine home, Hallelujah!
5. On de rock gwine home in Jesus' name, Hallelujah!
6. Michael boat a music boat, Hallelujah!
7. Gabriel blow de trumpet horn, Hallelujah!
8. O you mind your boastin' talk, Hallelujah!
9. Boastin' talk will sink your soul, Hallelujah!
10. Brudder, lend a helpin' hand, Hallelujah!
11. Sister, help for trim dat boat, Hallelujah!
12. Jordan stream is wide and deep, Hallelujah!
13. Jesus stand on t' oder side, Hallelujah!
14. I wonder if my maussa deh, Hallelujah!
15. My fader gone to unknown land, Hallelujah!
16. O de Lord he plant his garden deh, Hallelujah!

(Allen, Ware, and Garrison 1867, 23)

Prayer Focus: My goal, my aim is making it to that celestial shore called heaven.

BIOY: Song of Solomon 5-8 (209/156)

Psalm 75
"Mos' Done Toilin' Here"

HM—MOS' done toilin' here, O, bretheren,
Hm—Lord, I'm mos' done toilin' here.

1 I long to shout, I love to sing
   Mos' done toilin' here.
   I love to praise my heab'nly King,
   Mos' done toilin' here.
2 I ain't been to heab'n, but I been tol'
   Mos done toilin' here.
   De streets up dere am paved wid gol',
   Mos done toilin' here.

(Johnson and Johnson 1926, 140)

Prayer Focus: I give thanks to you, O God. I thank you that exaltation comes from you!

BIOY: Isaiah 1–4 (210/155)

Matthew 1-2
"My Army Cross Over"

1   MY brudder, tik keer Satan, My army cross ober,
    My brudder, tik keer Satan, My army cross ober.
2   Satan bery busy, ...
3   Wash 'e face in ashes, ...
4   Put on de leder apron, ...
5   Jordan riber rollin', ...
6   Cross 'em, I tell ye, cross 'em, ...
7   Cross Jordan (danger) riber, ...

Variation.
1   My army cross ober, My army cross ober,
    O Pharaoh's army drowned,
        My army cross ober,
    My army, my army, my army cross ober.
2   We'll cross de riber Jordan, ...
3   We'll cross de danger water, ...
4   We'll cross de mighty Myo, ...
                    (Allen, Ware, and Garrison 1867, 38)

Prayer Focus: Glory to the newborn King!

BIOY: Isaiah 5-7 (211/154)

Psalm 76
"My Body Rock 'Long Fever"

1   WAI', my brudder,* better true believe,†
    Better true be long time get over crosses;
    Wai', my sister, better true believe,
    An' 'e get up to heaven at last.
    O my body rock 'long fever,
    O! wid a pain in 'e head!
    I wish I been to de kingdom,
    to sit along side o' my Lord!

2   By de help ob de Lord we rise up again,
    O de Lord he comfort de sinner;
    By de help ob de Lord we rise up again,
    An' we'll get to heaven at last.

(Allen, Ware, and Garrison 1867, 32)

  * All de member
  † Long time seeker 'gin to believe.

Prayer Focus: When I'm discouraged and think my work's in vain, send your Spirit; revive me again!

BIOY: Isaiah 8-10 (212/153)

Matthew 3-4
"My Father, How Long?"
(Ps. 13:1-6)

MY father,* how long, My father, how long,
My father, how long, Poor sinner suffer here?

1   And it won't be long, (3x)
    Poor sinner suffer here.
2   We'll soon be free, (3x)
    De Lord will call us home.
3   We'll walk de miry road, (3x)
    Where pleasure never dies.
4   We'll walk de golden streets, (3x)
    Of de New Jerusalem.
5   My brudders do sing, (3x)
    De praises of de Lord.
6   We'll fight for liberty, (3x)
    When de Lord will call us home.

(Allen, Ware, and Garrison 1867, 93)

* Mother, etc.

Prayer Focus: How long, Lord? I was just wondering. I don't mean to hurry you. How long is, "Not long?"

Psalm 77
"My Good Lord's Been Here"

MY good Lord's been here,
Blest my soul and gone away;
My good Lord's been here,
Blest my soul and gone away.

1   Never did I think that He was so nigh,
    Blest my soul and gone away;
    He spoke and He made me laugh and cry,
    Blest my soul and gone away.

2   Sinner, better min' how you walk on the cross, ...
    Your foot might slip and your soul get lost, ...

(Boatner and Townsend 1927, 77)

Prayer Focus: Oh, Jesus, I can feel your presence. You're real. Your word is truth. It's good to trust you and obey. You walk with me, talk with me, and give me victory. I trust you. You are my joy in the midst of sorrow; my hope for tomorrow. Come into my life and stay, your commands I will obey.

BIOY: Isaiah 15-17 (214/151)

Matthew 5-6
"My Lord Says He's Gwinter Rain Down Fire"

1   MY Lord, (My Lord) My Lord, (My Lord) (2x)
    My Lord says he's gwinter rain down fire;
    My Lord, (My Lord) My Lord, (My Lord) (2x)
    My Lord says he's gwinter rain down,
    My Lord says he's gwinter rain down fire.

2   Gabriel, (Gabriel) Gabriel (Gabriel) (2x)
    Gabriel blow yo' silver trumpet; ...

3   Moses, (Moses) Moses (Moses) (2x)
    Moses smote de red Sea over; ...

4   Pharoah, (Pharoah) Pharoah, (Pharoah) (2x)
    Pharoah an' his host got drownded, ...

5   Peter, (Peter) Peter (Peter) (2x)
    Peter on de Sea o' Gallilee, ...

6   Take yo' (take yo') Take yo' (take yo') (2x)
    Take yo' net an' foller me, ...

(Johnson and Johnson 1926, 28)

Prayer Focus: Your wrath is kindled like fire and wax-es hot like molten rock for the Judgment Day.

BIOY: Isaiah 18-20 (215/150)

Psalm 78
"My Lord's a-Writin' All de Time"

1   COME down, come down, my Lord, come down,
My Lord's a-writin' all de time,
An' take me up to wear de crown,
My Lord's a-writin' all de time.

2   King Jesus rides in de middle of de air, …
He's callin' sinners from ev'ry where, …

3   Oh, He sees all you do, He hears all you say, …
Oh, He sees all you do, He hears all you say, …

4   When I was down in Egypt's lan', …
I heard some talk of de promised lan', …

5   Christians, you had better pray, …
For Satan's round you ev'ry day, …

Oh, He sees all you do, He hears all you say, …
Oh, He sees all you do, He hears all you say, …
(Johnson and Johnson 1925, 123)

Prayer Focus: Lord, forgive me. Please be patient with me. I am often forgetful of who you are and what you've done for me.

BIOY: Isaiah 21–23 (216/149)

Matthew 7-8
"My Lord, What a Mornin'"

MY Lord, what a mornin',
My Lord, what a mornin',
My Lord, what a mornin',
When de stars begin to fall. (repeat)

1   You'll hear de trumpet sound,
    To wake de nations under ground,
    Lookin' to my God's right hand,
    When de stars begin to fall.

2   You'll hear de sinner moan, ...

3   You'll hear de Christians shout, ...

(Johnson and Johnson 1925, 162)

Prayer Focus: Lord, you say, "Ask and it shall be given to you." My request is, "Not my will but, thy will be done." I want to enter the kingdom of heaven. Lord, help me to do the will of the Almighty.

BIOY: Isaiah 24-26 (217/148)

Psalm 79
"My Ship Is on de Ocean"

MY ship is on de ocean,
My ship is on de ocean,
My ship is on de ocean,
Po' sinner, fare-you-well.
1   I'm goin' away to see de good ol' Daniel,
    I'm goin' away to see my Lord,
    I'm goin' away to see de good ol' Daniel,
    I'm goin' away to see my Lord.
2   I'm goin' away to see de weepin' Mary, ...
    I'm goin' away to see de weepin' Mary, ...
                              (Johnson and Johnson 1926, 150)

Prayer Focus: Lord God, my love for you is like a ship sailing on an ocean of sin and temptation, carrying a cargo full of grace and mercy. I don't want to rock the boat. I don't want to tip this boat over. Jesus, you are the captain; sail me safely to the other side.

BIOY: Isaiah 27-29 (218/147)

Matthew 9–10
"My Soul's Been Anchored in de Lord"

IN de Lord, in de Lord,
My soul's been anchored in de Lord;
In de Lord, in de Lord,
My soul's been anchored in de Lord.

1   Befo' I'd stay in hell one day,
   My soul's been anchored in de Lord;
   I'd sing an' pray myself away,
   My soul's been anchored in de Lord,
   O, Lord, My soul's been anchored in de Lord,
   O, Lord, My soul's been anchored in de Lord.

2   I'm gwinter pray an' never stop,
   My soul's been anchored in de Lord;
   Until I reach de mountain top,
   My soul's been anchored in de Lord, …

                     (Johnson and Johnson 1926, 37)

Prayer Focus: Thank you for spiritual power.

BIOY: Isaiah 30–33 (219/146)

Psalm 80
"My Way's Cloudy"

O BRETHEREN, my way,
my way's cloudy, my way,
Go sen'-a dem angels down,

1 Dere's fire in de eas' an' fire in de wes',
Sen' dem angels down,
Dere's fire among dem Methodis',
Oh, sen'-a dem angels down.

2 Old Satan is mad an' I'm so glad, ...
He missed de soul he thought he had, ...

(Johnson and Johnson 1925, 92)

Prayer Focus: Problems to my right, problems to my left; everywhere I look problems keep coming in my way. Look down from heaven and see. Restore me, O God. Cause your face to shine and I will be delivered

BIOY: Isaiah 34-36 (220/145)

Matthew 11-12
"No Hiding Place"
(Rev. 6:15-16)

DOWN here, down here,
There's no hiding place down here,
Oh, I went to the rocks to hide my face,
The rocks cried out, "No hiding place,"
There's no hiding place down here.

1 Sinner man, you better repent,
   Sinner man, you better repent,
   Sinner man, you better repent,
   For God's going to call you to the judgment,
   There's no hiding place down here.

2 Sinner man, your heart's like steel, (3x)
   But the fire in hell's going to make you feel,
   There's no hiding place down here.

3 The sinner man gambled and fell, (3x)
   He wanted to go to heaven,
       but he had to go to hell,
   There's no hiding place down here.

(Boatner and Townsend 1927, 83)

Prayer Focus: Help me share the gospel with those who need to know the Good News.

BIOY: Isaiah 37-39 (221/144)

Psalm 81
"No Man Can Hinder Me"
(Ps. 118:6)

1 WALK in, kind Saviour, *No man can hinder me!*
  Walk in, sweet Jesus, *No man can hinder me!*
2 See what wonder Jesus done, ...
  See what wonder Jesus done, ...
  O no man, no man, no man can hinder me!
  O no man, no man, no man can hinder me!
3 Jesus make de dumb to speak, ...
4 Jesus make de cripple walk, ...
5 Jesus give de blind his sight, ...
6 Jesus do most anyting, ...
7 Rise, poor Lajarush, from de tomb, ...
8 Satan ride an iron-gray horse, ...
9 King Jesus ride a milk-white horse, ...

(Allen, Ware, and Garrison 1867, 10)

Prayer Focus: Lord, soon subdue my enemies and those who would do harm to your child.

BIOY: Isaiah 40-42 (222/143)

Matthew 13-14
"No More Rain Fall for Wet You"

1   NO more rain fall for wet you,
    Hallelu, hallelu,
    No more rain fall for wet you,
    Hallelujah.

2   No more sun shine for burn you, …

3   No more parting in de kingdom, …

4   No more backbiting in de kingdom, …

5   Every day shall be Sunday, …

(Allen, Ware, and Garrison 1867, 46)

Prayer Focus: Lord, oppressive systems and institutions have forced me to the outer fringes of society. I live in a socioeconomic box made of cardboard. Like a homeless vagabond, I weather the cold and rainy storms of this life wearing a coat of denied opportu-nity. You care and have prepared a place for me in the beautiful city of God. I'm grateful!

BIOY: Isaiah 43-46 (223/142)

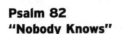

Psalm 82
"Nobody Knows"

OH! Nobody knows the trouble I've seen,
Nobody knows but Jesus;
Nobody knows the trouble I've seen,
Glory, hallelujah!

1   Sometimes I'm up, sometimes I'm down,
    Oh, yes, Lord!
    Sometimes I'm almost to the ground,
    Oh, yes, Lord! Oh!

2   Today you see me goin' 'long so, …
    But I have trials here below, …

3   The brightest day I ever saw, …
    When Jesus washed my sins away, …

(Boatner and Townsend 1927, 44)

Prayer Focus: Lord, I stand before judges, unjust judges who show partiality to the wicked. I cry unto you, like both the Hebrew and the African slaves. Remember me when I cry unto you.

BIOY: Isaiah 47–49 (224/141)

Matthew 15-16
"Nobody Knows de Trouble I See"

NOBODY knows de trouble I see, Lord,
Nobody knows de trouble I see,
Nobody knows de trouble I see, Lord,
Nobody knows like Jesus.

1   Brothers, will you pray for me,
    Brothers, will you pray for me,
    Brothers will you pray for me,
    An' help me to drive ole Satan away.

2   Mothers, will you pray for me,
    Mothers, will you pray for me,
    Mothers will you pray for me,
    An' help me to drive ole Satan away.

(Johnson and Johnson 1925, 140)

Prayer Focus: Lord, you are the Christ, the Son of the living God. You know all things and you have all power. Come, hear my cry. Chase my grief away.

BIOY: Isaiah 50-53 (225/140)

Psalm 83
"Nobody Knows the Trouble I've Had"

NOBODY knows de trouble I've had,*
Nobody knows but Jesus,
Nobody knows de trouble I've had,
Glory hallelu!

1   One morning I was a-walking down, O yes, Lord!
    I saw some berries a-hanging down, O yes, Lord!
    O yes, Lord! I saw some berries a-hanging down.

2   I pick de berry and I suck de juice, ...
    Just as sweet as the honey in de comb, ...

3   Sometimes I'm up, sometimes I'm down, ...
    Sometimes I'm almost on de groun', ...

4   What make ole Satan hate me so? ...
    Because he got me once and he let me go, ...

                    (Allen, Ware, and Garrison 1867, 55)

* I see

Prayer Focus: You are my deliverer. Set me free!

BIOY: Isaiah 54–57 (226/139)

Matthew 17-18
"None But the Righteous"

OH, none but the righteous,
None but the righteous,
None but the righteous shall see God.

1 Come, Thou fount of ev'ry blessing,
    Tune my heart to sing Thy praise;
Streams of mercy, never ceasing,
    Call for songs of loudest praise.

2 Here I raise my Ebenezer,
    Hither by Thy help I come;
And I hope, by Thy good pleasure,
    Safely to arrive at home.

3 Jesus sought me when a stranger,
    Wand'ring from the fold of God;
He, to rescue me from danger,
    Interposed His precious blood.

4 O to grace how great a debtor,
    Daily I'm constrained to be!
Let that grace, Lord, like a fetter,
    Bind my wand'ring heart to Thee.

(Boatner and Townsend 1927, 8)

Prayer Focus: Songs of praise I will ever sing to you.

BIOY: Isaiah 58-59 (227/138)

◎◎◎◎◎◎◎◎◎◎◎◎◎◎◎◎◎◎◎◎◎◎◎◎◎◎◎◎

Psalm 84
"Not Weary Yet"

O ME no weary yet, O me no weary yet.
1   I have a witness in my heart,
    O me no weary yet. (Brudder Tony*)
2   Since I been in de field to† fight, ...
3   I have a heaven to maintain, ...
4   De bond of faith are on my soul, ...
5   Ole Satan toss a ball at me, ...
6   Him tink de ball would hit my soul, ...
7   De ball for hell and I for heaven, ...
(Allen, Ware, and Garrison 1867, 12)

* Sister Mary.
† Been-a

Prayer Focus: Lord, I am determined to make heaven my home. I won't stop until I make it there.

BIOY: Isaiah 60-62 (228/137)

Matthew 19-20
"Now Is the Needy Time"

1   O now is the needy time,
*Now is the needy time, now is the needy time,
the needy time,
Now is the needy time, the needy time.*

2   Lord, won't you come by here? …
Come by here, …

3   Lord, won't you hear me pray? …
Hear me pray, …

4   Lord, won't you hear me groan? …
Hear me groan, …

(Boatner and Townsend 1927, 16)

Prayer Focus: If ever we needed you, we sure do need you now. Lord, won't you help my people? We need you so.

BIOY: Isaiah 63-66 (229/136)

Psalm 85
"O Brothers, Don't Get Weary"

1   O BROTHERS, don't get weary,
     O brothers, don't get weary,
     O brothers, don't get weary,
     We're waiting for the Lord.
2   We'll land on Canaan's shore,
     We'll land on Canaan's shore,
     When we land on Canaan's shore,
     We'll meet forever more.

(Allen, Ware, and Garrison 1867, 95)

Prayer Focus: Lord, no good thing will you withhold from those who walk upright. I actively wait for truth and mercy to meet, justice and love to kiss, and joy and peace to walk hand in hand in Canaan land. A gentle breeze of delight shall always be just right upon the celestial shore, with peace forever more. Lord, you give good gifts to your children. Thank you.

BIOY: Jeremiah 1–3 (230/135)

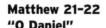

Matthew 21-22
"O Daniel"

YOU call yourself church-member,
You hold your head so high,
You praise God with your glitt'ring tongue,
But you leave all your heart behind.
O my Lord delivered Daniel,
O Daniel, O Daniel,
O my Lord delivered Daniel,
O why not deliver me too?

(Allen, Ware, and Garrison 1867, 94)

Prayer Focus: O my Lord, Satan's lynch mob is after me again! Daily angels of darkness—calling themselves church members—torment, torture, and torch the righteous. They lynch, mutilate, and cut body parts for souvenirs. So much pain, sorrow, and agony to be free! O my Lord, you delivered Daniel, why not deliver me, too? "Oh God, help me Jesus!"

BIOY: Jeremiah 4-6 (231/134)

Psalm 86
"O Mary, Don't You Weep"

O MARY, don't you weep, don't you mourn,
O Mary, don't you weep, don't you mourn;
Pharoh's army got drownded,
O Mary, don't you weep.

1 Some of these mornings bright and fair,
 Take my wings and cleave the air.
 Pharoh's army got drownded
 O Mary, don't you weep.

2 When I get to Heaven goin' to sing and shout,
 Nobody there for to turn me out, ...

3 When I get to Heaven goin' to put on my shoes,
 Run about glory and tell all the news, ...
 (The AME Zion Bicentennial Hymnal 1996, 618)

Prayer Focus: Bow down your ear, O Lord. Teach me your way. Preserve my life. O Lord, rejoice my soul and give me a heart to praise you.

BIOY: Jeremiah 7-9 (232/133)

Matthew 23-24
"O My Lord, What Shall I Do?"

1   SOON one morning
death came creeping in my room,
Soon one morning
death came creeping in my room,
Soon one morning
death came creeping in my room;
O my Lord, O my Lord, what shall I do?

2   Soon one morning
death took my mother away, (3x)
O my Lord, O my Lord, what shall I do?

3   Soon one morning
Death took my father away, (3x)
O my Lord, O my Lord, what shall I do?

4   Soon one morning
death took my sister away, (3x)
O my Lord, O my Lord, what shall I do?

(Boatner and Townsend 1927, 19)

Prayer Focus: I will trust in you, Lord, 'til I die!

BIOY: Jeremiah 10-12 (233/132)

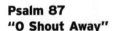

Psalm 87
"O Shout Away"

O SHOUT, O shout away,
And don't you mind,
And glory, glory, glory in my soul!

1   And when 'twas night I thought 'twas day,
    I thought I'd pray my soul away,
    And glory, glory, glory in my soul!

2   Satan told me not to pray,
    He want my soul at judgment day, ...

3   And every where I went to pray,
    There some thing was in my way, ...

(Allen, Ware, and Garrison 1867, 71)

Prayer Focus: Lord, I've found the answer to all my problems—I've learned to pray! All of my sins are forgiven. I'm free of my cares. O, sweet hour of prayer, that calls me from a world of care! I've learned to bring my problems to your altar and leave them there.

BIOY: Jeremiah 13-15 (234/131)

Matthew 25-26
"O'er the Crossing"

1 BENDIN' knees a-achin', Body racked wid pain,
  I wish I was a child of God, I'd git home bime-bye.
  Keep prayin', *I do believe*
  We're a long time waggin' o' de crossin';
  Keep prayin', I do believe
  We'll git home to heaven bime-bye.
2 O yonder's my ole mudder,
      Been a waggin' at de hill so long;
  It's about time she cross over, Git home bime-bye,
  Keep prayin', *I do believe,* …
3 O hear dat lumberin' thunder A-roll
      from do' to do',
  A-callin' de people home to God;
      Dey'll git home bime-bye.
  Little Chil'n, *I do believe,* …
4 O see dat forked lightnin' A-jump
      from cloud to cloud,
  A-pickin' up God's chil'n;
      Dey'll git home bime-bye.
  Pray mourner, *I do believe,* …
                    (Allen, Ware, and Garrison 1867, 72)

Prayer Focus: Bye and bye we'll make it home.

BIOY: Jeremiah 16-18 (235/130)

◎◎◎◎◎◎◎◎◎◎◎◎◎◎◎◎◎◎◎◎◎◎◎◎◎◎

Psalm 88
"O, Gambler, Git Up Off o' Yo' Knees"

1 O, GAMBLER, git up off o' yo' knees,
    O, gambler, git up off o' yo' knees,
    O, gambler, git up off o' yo' knees,
2 End o' dat mornin', Good Lord.
    End o' dat mornin', Good Lord,
    End o' dat mornin' when de Lord said to hurry.
3 O, gambler, you can't a-ride on dis train,
    O, gambler, you can't a-ride on dis train,
    O, gambler, you can't a-ride on dis train,
4 End o' dat mornin', Good Lord.
    End o' dat mornin', Good Lord,
    End o' dat mornin' when de Lord said to hurry.

(Johnson and Johnson 1925, 122)

Prayer Focus: "Lord, are you listening? I'd like earthly riches untold. Are you listening? If only I had more money, ... then ...." Often, I've prayed foolishly and lied to you and to myself. You heard? Mercy! Work on my mind, my tongue, and my heart.

BIOY: Jeremiah 19-22 (236/129)

Matthew 27-28
"O, Rocks Don't Fall on Me"

O, ROCKS, don't fall on me,
  O, rocks, don't fall on me,
O, rocks, don't fall on me,
Rocks an' mountains don't fall on me,
I'm praying O, rocks, don't fall on me,
O, rocks, don't fall on me,
  O, rocks, don't fall on me,
Rocks an' mountains don't fall on me,

1 I look ovah yondah on Jericho's walls,
   Rocks an' mountains don't fall on me,
   An' see dem sinners tremble an' fall,
   Rocks an' mountains don't fall on me.

2 O in-a dat great great judg-a-ment day, …
   De sinners will run to de rocks an say, …

3 When ey-ah-ry star refuses to shine, …
   I know dat King Jesus will-a be mine, …

4 De trumpet shall soun' An' de dead shall rise, …
   An' go to de mansions in-a de skies, … .

(Johnson and Johnson 1925, 164)

Prayer Focus: With great eagerness I look forward to Judgment Day.

BIOY: Jeremiah 23-25 (237/128)

Psalm 89
"O, Wasn't Dat a Wide River?"

O, WASN'T dat a wide river,
dat river of Jordan, Lord, Wide river!
Dere's one mo' river to cross.

1   O, de river of Jordan is so wide,
     One mo' river to cross.
     I don't know how to get on de other side;
     One mo' river to cross.

2   Ol' Satan am nothin' but a snake in de grass, ...
     If you ain't mighty careful he will hol' you fas'; ...

(Johnson and Johnson 1925, 152)

Prayer Focus: Lord, seems like just living this life is like crossing over the Jordan. Crossing over the wide river Jordan is a lifelong journey. "Lord, when I tread the verge of Jordan, bid my anxious fears subside. Bear me through the swelling current; land me safe on Canaan's side."

BIOY: Jeremiah 26-28 (238/127)

Mark 1-2
"You'd Better Min'"

1 YOU'D better min' how you talk,
   You'd better min' what you talkin' about,
   You got to give account in de Judgment,
   You'd better min'.
   You'd better min', you'd better min',
   You got to give account in de Judgment,
   You'd better min'.

2 You'd better min' how you sing,
   you'd better min' what you singin' about, ...

3 You'd better min' how you shout,
   you'd better min' what you shoutin' about, ...

(Songs of Zion 1981, 125)

Prayer Focus: Lord, help me to have a walk worthy of the calling with which I have been called, with all lowliness, gentleness, and longsuffering, bearing with one another in love, endeavoring to keep the unity of the Spirit in the bond of peace.

BIOY: Jeremiah 29-31 (239/126)

Psalm 90
"Oh, My Good Lord, Show Me de Way"

OH, my good Lord, show me de way,
Oh, my good Lord, show me de way,
Oh, my good Lord, show me de way,
Enter de chariot, travel along.
1 Ol' Noah sent out a mournin' dove,
 Enter de chariot, travel along.
 Which brought back a token of-a heab'nly love
 Enter de chariot, travel along.
2 Gwinter serve my God while I have breath, …
 So I kin see my Jesus after death, …
3 When I get to heab'n gwine put on my shoes, …
 I'll walk all over heab'n an' spread de news, …

(Johnson and Johnson 1926, 133)

Prayer Focus: Swing low, sweet chariot, and let me ride. O, let me ride! I'll wave good bye. Watch my life pass on by, as I ride to the beautiful city of God.

BIOY: Jeremiah 32-35 (240/125)

🔘🔘🔘🔘🔘🔘🔘🔘🔘🔘🔘🔘🔘🔘🔘🔘🔘🔘🔘🔘

Mark 3-4
"Oh, Yes! Oh, Yes! Wait 'til I Git on My Robe"

1   I COME dis night to sing an' pray,
        Oh, yes, Oh, yes,
    To drive ol' Satan far away, *Oh, yes, Oh, yes.*

2   Dat heav'nly home is bright an' fair,
        Oh, yes, Oh, yes,
    But mighty few can enter dere, *Oh, yes, Oh, yes,*
    Oh, wait 'til I git on my robe,
        wait 'til I git on my robe,
    Wait 'til I git on my robe, Oh, yes, Oh, yes.

3   Oh, I went down in de valley to pray, ...
    I met ol' Satan on de way, ...

4   An' if you wanter catch dat heab'nly breeze, ...
    Go down in de valley on yo' knees an' pray, ...

5   Now what do you think he said to me, ...
    You're too young to pray an' too young to die, ...

6   Oh, bow yo' knees up on de groun', ...
    An' ask yo' Lord to turn you 'roun', ...

(Johnson and Johnson 1926, 105)

Prayer Focus: I'm crossing over (cf. Mark 4:35–41). I just can't wait 'til I get on my robe!

BIOY: Jeremiah 36-38 (241/124)

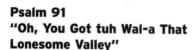

Psalm 91
"Oh, You Got tuh Wal-a That Lonesome Valley"

1. OH you got tuh walk-a
that lonesome valley,
You got tuh go tha by yo'self,
No one heah to go tha with you,
You got to go tha by yo'self.

2. Jurdun's stream
is cold and chilly,
You got tuh wade it faw yo'self,
No one heah tuh wade it faw you,
You got tuh wade it faw yo'self.

3. When my dear Lawd
was hangin' bleedin',
He had tuh hang tha by His-self,
No one tha could hang tha faw Him,
He had tuh hang tha by His-self.

4. When you reach
the rivah Jurdun,
You got tuh cross it by yo'self,
No one heah may cross it with you,
You got tuh cross it by yo'self.

"Oh, You Got tuh Wal-a That Lonesome Valley" (cont.)

5   When you face
     that Judgmunt mawnin',
    You got tuh face it by yo'self,
    No one heah tuh face it faw you,
    You got tuh face it by yo'self.
6   You got tuh stan' yo'
     trial in Judgmunt,
    You got tuh stan' it by yo'self,
    No one heah tuh stan' it faw you,
    You got tuh stan' it by yo'self.

(Lovell 1972, 273)

Prayer Focus: Give me courage to stand alone. Yet I know that I am never really alone. You are always by my side.

BIOY: Jeremiah 39-42 (242/123)

Mark 5-6
"Old Time Religion"

'TIS the old time religion,
   'Tis the old time religion,
'Tis the old time religion,
   And it's good enough for me.

1   It was good for our mothers, (3x)
   And it's good enough for me.
2   Makes me love ev'rybody, (3x) ...
3   It has saved our fathers, (3x) ...
4   It was good for the prophet Daniel, (3x) ...
5   It was good for the Hebrew children, (3x) ...
6   It was tried in the fiery furnace, (3x) ...
7   It was good for Paul and Silas, (3x) ...
8   It will do when I am dying, (3x) ....

(The New National Baptist Hymnal 1977, 505)

Prayer Focus: Lord, revive in us that old time religion!
Let us feel your presence deep within our souls.

BIOY: Jeremiah 43-45 (243/122)

Psalm 92
"On Calvary"

ON Calvary, On Calvary,
On Calvary, On Calvary,
Oh see how He died on Calvary.

1 O bring me the basin
Let me wash my hands,
I won't be guilty
Of this innocent man,
Oh see how He died on Calvary.

2 O the blood ran down
From His wounded side,
O the blood ran down
From His wounded side, *Oh see ...*

3 He died for you And He died for me,
He died for you And He died for me, *Oh see ...*

(Boatner and Townsend 1927, 69)

Prayer Focus: We who believe have redemption through your blood!

BIOY: Jeremiah 46-48 (244/121)

Mark 7-8
"On Ma Journey"

ON ma journey now, Mount Zion,
On ma journey now, Mount Zion,
Well I wouldn't take nothin', Mount Zion,
for ma journey now; Mount Zion.

1 One day, one day I was walking a long,
 Well, the elements opened
 an' de love come down, Mount Zion.

2 I went to de valley an' I didn't go to stay,
 Well, my soul got happy
 an' I stayed all day, Mount Zion.

3 Just talk about me, just as much as you please,
 Well, I'll talk about you,
 when I bend my knees, Mount Zion.

(Songs of Zion 1981, 157)

Prayer Focus: Down on bended knee, it is my earnest plea to love thee with all that is in me.

BIOY: Jeremiah 49-52 (245/120)

DAY 246

Psalm 93
"On to Glory"

1   O COME my brethren and sisters too,
 We're gwine to join the heavenly crew;
 To Christ our Saviour let us sing,
 And make our loud hosannas ring.
 O hallelu, O hallelu
 O hallelujah to the Lord.

2   Oh, there's Bill Thomas, I know him well,
 He's got to work to keep from hell;
 He's got to pray by night and day,
 If he wants to go by the narrow way.

3   There's Chloe Williams, she makes me mad,
 For you see I know she's going on bad;
 She told me a lie this arternoon,
 And the devil will get her very soon.

     (Allen, Ware, and Garrison 1867, 66)

Prayer Focus: Holiness adorns your house!

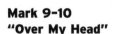

Mark 9–10
"Over My Head"

OVER my head I see trouble in the air,
Over my head I see trouble in the air,
Over my head I see trouble in the air,
There must be a God somewhere.

1   Over my head I see music in the air, (3x)
    There must be a God somewhere.
2   Over my head I see color in the air, (3x)
    There must be a God somewhere.
3   Over my head I see glory in the air, (3x)
    There must be a God somewhere.
              (The New National Baptist Hymnal 1977, 510)

Prayer Focus: Thank you for eyes that see your awesome wondrous beauty; for ears that hear of your miraculous power; for a mind that understands the mystery (Col. 1:26–27); and, enough sense to know there must be a God somewhere! My Lord, my God!

BIOY: Lamentations 4–5 (247/118)

Psalm 94
"Peter, Go Ring Dem Bells"

OH, Peter, go ring dem bells,
Peter, go ring dem bells,
Peter, go ring dem bells,
I heard f 'om heav'n today.

1   I wonder where my mother is gone, (3x)
I heard f 'om heav'n today, (3x)
I thank God an' I thank you too,
I heard f 'om heav'n today.
Oh, Peter, go ring dem bells,
Peter, go ring dem bells, (2x)
I heard f 'om heav'n today, (3x)
It's good news an' I thank God too,
I heard f 'om heav'n today.
Oh, Peter, go ring dem bells,
Peter, go ring dem bells, (2x)
I heard f 'om heav'n today, (2x)

2   I wonder where Sister Mary is gone, (3x)
I heard f 'om heav'n today, (3x) …

(Johnson and Johnson 1925, 137)

Prayer Focus: O Lord, my God and Judge, I'm glad I heard that vengeance belongs to you, not me (Ps. 94:1–2).

BIOY: Ezekiel 1-4 (248/117)

Mark 11
"Plenty Good Room"

THERE'S plenty good room, plenty good room,
plenty good room in ma Father's kingdom,
Plenty good room, plenty good room,
just choose your seat and sit down.

1   I would not be a sinner,
    I'll tell you the reason why;
    I'm afraid my Lord might call on me,
    and I wouldn't be ready to die.

2   I would not be a liar, ...

3   I would not be a cheater, ...

(Songs of Zion 1981, 99)

Prayer Focus: There's room at the cross for me? Though millions have come, yet there's still room for one? O God, again I stand beneath that fountain filled with blood, drawn from Immanuel's veins. Wash me, cleanse me, rinse away the stain of my sin.

BIOY: Ezekiel 5-7 (249/116)

Psalm 95
"Po' Mourner's Got a Home at Las'"

HM, Hm, my Lord!
Hm, Po' mourner's got a home at las'.

1   Mourner, mourner, Ain't you tired o' mournin';
    Bow down on-a yo' knees
    an' join de ban' wid de angels.
    O, no harm, Lord, no harm,
    Go tell brudder Elijah,
    No harm, Lord, no harm,
    Po' mourner's got a home at las'.

2   Sinner, sinner, Ain't you tired o' sinnin', …

3   O, gambler, gambler, Ain't you tired o' gamblin', …
                                    (Johnson and Johnson 1926, 78)

Prayer Focus: Lord, I'm tired. May I enter your rest?

BIOY: Ezekiel 8-10 (250/115)

Luke 1-2
"Poor Rosy"

1   POOR Rosy, poor gal;*
Poor Rosy, poor gal;
Rosy break my poor heart,
Heav'n shall-a be my home.
I cannot stay in hell one day,
Heav'n shall-a be my home;
I'll sing and pray my soul away,
Heav'n shall-a be my home.

2   Got hard trial in my way, (ter)
Heav'n shall-a be my home.
O when I talk,† I talk† wid God,
Heav'n shall-a be my home. (bis)

3   I dunno what de people‡ want of me, (ter)
Heav'n shall-a be my home.

(Allen, Ware, and Garrison 1867, 7)

   * Poor Caesar, poor boy.
   † Walk.
   ‡ Massa.

Prayer Focus: I'm determined to make heaven my home. Lord, with you as my leader, I'll make it there someday.

BIOY: Ezekiel 11-13 (251/114)

Psalm 96
"Praise, Member"

PRAISE, member,* praise God,
I praise my Lord until I die;
Praise, member, praise God,†
And reach de heavenly home.‡

1   O Jordan's bank§ is a good old bank,
   And I hain't but one more river to cross;
   I want some valiant soldier
   To help me bear the cross.

2   O soldier's fight is a good old fight, ...

3   O I look to de East, and I look to de West, ...

4   O I wheel to de right, and I wheel to de left, ...

(Allen, Ware, and Garrison 1867, 4)

* Believer.
† Religion so sweet.
‡ Shore.
§ Stream, Fight.

Prayer Focus: Lord, you are great and greatly to be praised (Ps. 96:4)! Honor and majesty to you.

BIOY: Ezekiel 14–17 (252/113)

Luke 3-4
"Pray all de Member"

1 PRAY all de member,* *O Lord!*
   Pray all de member, *Yes, my Lord!*
2 Pray a little longer, ...
3 Jericho da worry me, ...
4 Jericho, Jericho, ...
5 I been to Jerusalem, ...
6 Patrol aroun' me, ...
7 Tank God he no ketch me, ...
8 Went to de meetin', ...
9 Met brudder Hacless [Hercules], ...
10 Wha' d'ye tink he tell me? ...
11 Tell me for to turn back, ...
12 Jump along Jericho, ...

(Allen, Ware, and Garrison 1867, 35)

* True Believer

Prayer Focus: Spirit of the Lord, be upon me.

BIOY: Ezekiel 18-20 (253/112)

Psalm 97
"Pray On"

PRAY on, pray on;
Pray on dem light us over;
Pray on, Pray on,
De union break of day.
My sister, you come to see baptize,
In de union break of day;
My 'loved sister,
you come to see baptize,
In de union break of day.

(Allen, Ware, and Garrison 1867, 97)

Prayer Focus: I love you, Lord. O how I hate evil! Preserve my soul. Deliver my brothers and sisters from the hand of the wicked. Let your light shine in the hearts of your people. With gladness I rejoice in you and give thanks at the remembrance of your holy name! I glorify, magnify, and praise you!

BIOY: Ezekiel 21–23 (254/111)

Luke 5-6
"Rain Fall and Wet Becca Lawton"

RAIN fall and wet* Becca Lawton,†
Oh, Rain fall and wet Becca Lawton,
Oh! Brudder‡ cry holy!

1 Been§ back holy,
   I must come slowly;
   Oh! Brudder cry holy!

2 Do, Becca Lawton, come to me yonder,

3 Say, brudder Tony, what shall I do now?

4 Beat back holy, and rock salvation.

          (Allen, Ware, and Garrison 1867, 21)

  * Sun come and dry.
  † All de member, &c.
  ‡ We all, Bekuever, & c.
  § Beat, Bent, Rack.

Prayer Focus: In everything that I do, remind me of you. Remind me that you are with me always.

BIOY: Ezekiel 24-26 (255/110)

Psalm 98
"Religion Is a Fortune
I Really Do Believe"

1   OH, religion is a fortune, *I really do believe,*
    Oh, religion is a fortune, *I really do believe,*
    Oh, religion is a fortune, *I really do believe,*
    Where Sabbaths have no end.

2   Gwinter sit down in de kingdom, *I really do believe,*
    Gwinter sit down in de kingdom, *I really do believe,*
    Gwinter walk about in Zion, *I really do believe,*
    Where Sabbaths have no end.
    Where you been po' mourner (sinner),
        where you been so long;
    Blow low down in de valley for to pray,
        An' I ain't done prayin' yet.

3   Gwinter See my Sister Mary, ...
    Gwinter see ol' Brudder Jonah, ...

4   Gwinter Walk-a wid de Angels, ...
    Gwinter see my Massa Jesus, ...
                        (Johnson and Johnson 1926, 53)

Prayer Focus: I really do believe. Lord, I have taken the
leap of faith. I will trust and obey today!

BIOY: Ezekiel 27–30 (256/109)

Luke 7-8
"Religion so Sweet"

1 O WALK Jordan long road, *And religion so sweet;*
2 O religion is good for anything, ...
3 Religion make you happy,* ...
4 Religion gib me patience,† ...
5 O member, get religion, ...
6 I long time been a-huntin', ...
7 I seekin' for my fortune, ...
8 O I gwine to meet my Savior, ...
9 Gwine to tell him 'bout my trials, ...
10 Dey call me boastin' member, ...
11 Dey call me turnback‡ Christian, ...
12 Dey call me 'struction maker, ...
13 But I don't care what dey call me, ...
14 Lord, trial 'longs to a Christian, ...
15 O tell me 'bout religion, ...
16 I weep for Mary and Marta, ...
17 I seek my Lord and I find him, ...

(Allen, Ware, and Garrison 1867, 13)

* Humble.
† Honor, Comfort.
‡ Lyin', 'ceitful.

Prayer Focus: Sweet Holy Spirit, fill my cup.

BIOY: Ezekiel 31-33 (257/108)

Psalm 99
"Ride On King Jesus"

RIDE on, King Jesus,
No man can a-hinder me,
Ride on, King Jesus, ride on,
No man can a-hinder me.

1 I was but young when I begun,
No man can a-hinder me,
But now my race is almost done,
No man can a-hinder me.

2 King Jesus rides on a milk-white horse, ...
The river of Jordan he did cross, ...

3 If you want to find your way to God, ...
The gospel highway must be trod, ...

(Songs of Zion 1981, 77)

Prayer Focus: Lord, who will dare to stand before me when I call on your great name (cf. Matt. 10:28)? Jesus, precious Savior, you give me victory!

Luke 9-10
"Ride on, Moses"

1   I'VE been travlin' all de day,
     Ride on, Moses,
     To hearde good folks sing an' pray;
     I want to go home in de mawnin'.

2   Dey pray'd so long I could not wait,
     Ride on, Moses,
     I know de Lord would pass dat way,
     I want to go home in de mawnin'. (Den)
     Ride on, ride on, ride on, Moses
     Ride on, King Emanual,
     I want to go home in de mawnin'.

(Johnson and Johnson 1925, 70)

Prayer Focus: Please provide me with a daily portion of love—that I may seek to understand and love others as myself; and strength to bear my cross.

BIOY: Ezekiel 37-39 (259/106)

Psalm 100
"Rise an' Shine"

OH, rise an' shine an' give God de glory, glory,
Rise an' shine an' give God de glory, glory,
Rise an' shine an' give God de glory, glory,
For de year ob Juberlee.

1 Jesus carry de young lambs in his bosom, bosom,
   Carry de young lambs in his bosom, bosom, (2x) …
   Jesus lead de ole sheep by still waters, waters,
   Lead de ole sheep by still waters, waters, (2x) …

2 Oh, come on mourners, get you ready, ready,
   Come on, mourners, get you ready, ready, (2x) …
   You may keep your lamps trimmed
        an' burning, burning,
   Keep your lamps, trimmed
        an' burning, burning, (2x) …

3 Oh, come on, children, don't be weary, weary,
   Come on children, don't be weary, weary, (2x) …
   Oh, don't you hear dem bells a-ringin', ringin',
   Don't you hear dem bells a-ringin', ringin', (2x)…
                (The AME Zion Bicentennial Hymnal 1996, 613)

Prayer Focus: I enter your presence with thanksgiving!

BIOY: Ezekiel 40-43 (260/105)

Luke 11–12
"Rise Up Shepherd an' Foller"
(Luke 2:15)

1   DERE'S a star in de Eas' on Christmas morn,
    Rise up Shepherd an' foller,
    It will lead to de place where de Saviour's born;
    Rise up Shepherd an' foller.
    Leave yo' flocks an' leave yo' lam's,
    Rise up Shepherd an' foller, foller,
    Leave yo' sheep an' leave yo' rams,
    Rise up Shepherd an' foller, yes, foller,
    Foller, foller, rise up Shepherd an' foller,
    Foller, de star of Bethlehem,
    Rise up Shepherd an' foller.

2   If you take good heed to de Angel's word, …
    You'll forget yo' flock you'll forget yo' herd, …

(Johnson and Johnson 1926, 66)

Prayer Focus: Jesus, you are so wonderful to me. I will rise up and follow you always.

BIOY: Ezekiel 44–46 (261/104)

Psalm 101
"Rise, Mourner, Rise"

1 RISE, mourner, rise, mourner,
   Oh, can't you rise an' tell what
   de Lord has done for you?
2 Rise, seeker, rise, seeker,
   Oh, can't you rise an' tell what
   de Lord has done for you?
3 Rise, sinner, rise, sinner,
   Oh, can't you rise an' tell what
   de Lord has done for you?
   Yes he's taken my feet out of de mi'ry clay,
   An' he's placed 'em on de right side of my Father.
   Yes he's taken my feet out of de mi'ry clay,
   An' he's placed 'em on de right side of my Father.
                     (Johnson and Johnson 1926, 116)

Prayer Focus: I just can't keep it to myself what you have done for me. I got a testimony!

BIOY: Ezekiel 47–48 (262/103)

Luke 13–14
"Rise, Shine, for Thy Light Is a-Coming"

OH, rise, shine, for thy light is a-coming,
Rise, shine, for thy light is a-coming,
Oh, rise, shine, for thy light is a-coming,
My Lord says He's coming by 'nd by.

1 Oh, wet or dry, I intend to try,
   My Lord says He's coming by an' by,
   To serve the Lord until I die,
   My Lord says He's coming by 'nd by.

2 We'll build our tent on this campground, …
   And give old Satan another round, …

3 I intend to shout and never stop, …
   Until I reach the mountain top, …

(Boatner and Townsend 1927, 42)

Prayer Focus: I celebrate, with the angels in heaven, everyone who repents this day (Luke 15:7). Here am I; use me to deliver someone this day.

BIOY: Daniel 1–4 (263/102)

Psalm 102
"Rock o' Jubilee"

1 O ROCK o' jubilee, poor fallen soul,*
   O Lord,† de rock o' jubilee!
2 O rock o' jubilee, and I rock'em all about,
   O Lord, de rock o' jubilee!
3 Stand back, Satan, let me come by, …
4 O come, titty Katy, let me go, …
5 I have no time for stay at home, …
6 My Fader door wide open now, …
7 Mary, girl, you know my name, …
8 Look dis way an' you look dat way, …
9 De wind blow East, he blow from Jesus, …
                    (Allen, Ware, and Garrison 1867, 25)

   * To mercy seat, To de corner o' de world.
   † Yes.

Prayer Focus: Look down from the heights of your sanctuary, O Lord. Hear my humble cry. While on others thou are calling, please do not pass me by.

BIOY: Daniel 5-8 (264/101)

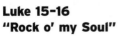

Luke 15-16
"Rock o' my Soul"
(Luke 16:19-31)

1   ROCK o' my soul in de bosom of Abraham,
    Rock o' my soul in de bosom of Abraham,
    Rock o' my soul in de bosom of Abraham,
    Lord, Rock o' my soul.

2   He toted the young lambs in his bosom,
    He toted the young lambs in his bosom,
    He toted the young lambs in his bosom,
    And leave the old sheep alone.

(Allen, Ware, and Garrison 1867, 73)

Prayer Focus: Lord, when I die I know where I want to go. Therefore, I know that I must now live a certain way. Help me to live according to your way. I submit myself to you. Help me to grow in spiritual truth and wisdom. Grant me spiritual discernment and power for spiritual warfare. I will use my gifts to promote your kingdom and support your church.

BIOY: Daniel 9-12 (265/100)

Psalm 103
"Rockin' Jerusalem"

O MARY, O Martha,
O Mary, ring dem bells,
O Mary, O Martha,
O Mary, ring dem bells,
I hear archangels a-rockin' Jerusalem,
I hear archangels a-ringin' dem bells.

1 Church gettin' higher! *Rockin' Jerusalem!*
   Church gettin' higher! *Ringin' dem bells.*

2 Listen to the lambs! ...
   Listen to the lambs! ...

3 New Jerusalem! ...
   New Jerusalem! ...

(Songs of Zion 1981, 103)

Prayer Focus: I bless, adore, and thank you with rhythm and song from the depths of my soul.

BIOY: Hosea 1-3 (266/99)

Luke 17-18
"Roll Jordan, Roll"

ROLL Jordan, roll, Roll Jordan, roll,
I wanter go to heav'n when I die,
To hear ol' Jordan roll.

1 Oh, brothers you oughter been dere,
   Yes my Lord
   A-sittin' up in de kingdom,
   To hear ol' Jordan roll.

2 Oh, sinner you oughter been dere,
   Yes my Lord
   A-sittin' up in de kingdom,
   To hear ol' Jordan roll.

(Johnson and Johnson 1925, 105)

Prayer Focus: "The things which are impossible with men are possible with God" (Luke 18:27). Lord, I'm looking for a miracle; expecting the impossible!

BIOY: Hosea 4-7 (267/98)

Psalm 104
"Roll, Jordan, Roll"

1   MY brudder* sittin' on de tree of life,
An' he yearde when Jordan roll;
Roll, Jordan, Roll, Jordan, Roll, Jordan, roll!
O march de angel march,
O march de angel march;
O my soul a-rise in Heaven, Lord,
For to yearde when Jordan roll.

2   Little chil'en learn to fear de Lord,
And let your days be long; ...

3   O, let no false nor spiteful word,
Be found upon your tongue; ...

(Allen, Ware, and Garrison 1867, 1)

  * Parson Fuller, Deacon Henshaw, Brudder Mosey,
Massa Linkum, &c.

Prayer Focus: When I get to heaven can I sit on the Tree of Life and watch the angels march and parade?

BIOY: Hosea 8-10 (268/97)

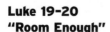
Luke 19-20
"Room Enough"

1 OH, brothers, *don't stay away,*
   Brothers, *don't stay away,*
   Brothers *don't stay away, Don't stay away.*
   For my Lord says, *there's room enough,*
   Room enough in the heav'ns for you,
   My Lord says, *there's room enough,*
   Don't stay away.

2 Oh, mourners, ... For the Bible says, ...

3 Oh, sinners, ... The angel says, ...

4 Oh, children, ... For Jesus says, ...

(Boatner and Townsend 1927, 53)

Prayer Focus: You saw Zacchaeus; do you see me?

BIOY: Hosea 11-14 (269/96)

Psalm 105
"Run, Mary, Run"

RUN, Mary, run, Run, Mary, run, Oh, run, Mary, run,
I know de udder worl' is not like dis.

1   Fire in de Eas' an' fire in de Wes',
      I know de udder worl' is not like dis.
    Boun' to burn de wilderness,
      I know de udder worl' is not like dis.

2   Jordan's river is a river to cross, ...
      Stretch yo' rod an' come across, ...

3   Swing low sweet chariot into de Eas', ...
      Let God's children have some peace, ...

4   Swing low sweet chariot into de Wes', ...
      Let God's children have some res', ...

5   Swing low sweet chariot into de Norf, ...
      Give me de gol' widout de dross, ...

6   Swing low sweet chariot into de Sout', ...
      Let God's children sing and shout, ...

7   Now if dis was de judgment day, ...
      Ev'ry sinner would want to pray, ...

8   Ol' trouble it come like a gloomy cloud, ...
      Gader thick an' thunder loud, ...

                                    (Johnson and Johnson 1926, 110)

Prayer Focus: Lord, I'm so glad to know you have prepared another place for me that is nothing like this
world. Thank you for loving me so!

BIOY: Joel 1-3 (270/95)

Luke 21-22
"Sabbath Has No End"

1   GWINE to walk about Zion, *I really do believe;*
    Walk about Zion, *I really do believe;*
    Walk about Zion, *I really do believe;*
    Sabbath has no end.
    I did view one angel In one angel stand;
    Let's mark him right down with the forehalf,
    With the harpess in his hand.
2   Gwine to follow King Jesus, I really do believe, …
3   I love God certain, I really do believe, …
4   My sister's got religion, I really do believe, …
5   Set down in the kingdom, I really do believe, …
6   Religion is a fortune, I really do believe, …

(Allen, Ware, and Garrison 1867, 69)

Prayer Focus: Father, if it is your will, remove this cross from me. Nevertheless, your will, not mine, be done.

BIOY: Amos 1-2 (271/94)

Psalm 106
"Sail, O Believer"

SAIL, O believer, sail,
Sail over yonder;
Sail, O my brudder, sail,
Sail over yonder.

(Allen, Ware, and Garrison 1867, 24)

Prayer Focus: "Remember me, O Lord, with the favor You have toward Your people; Oh visit me with Your salvation, That I may see the benefit of your chosen ones, That I may rejoice in the gladness of Your nation, That I may glory with Your inheritance" (Ps. 106:4–5). I have sinned. I have committed iniquity. I have behaved wickedly. I have rebelled. Have mercy on me, O Lord. In spite of my iniquities, save me for your name's sake that you might make your mighty power known. Redeem me from my enemies and I will give thanks to your holy name and triumph in your praise.

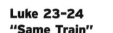

Luke 23-24
"Same Train"

1 SAME train, same train,
   Same train, carry my mother,
   Same train, same train,
   Same train carry my mother,
   Same train be back tomorrer.
2 Same train, same train,
   Same train, carry my sister,
   Same train, same train,
   Same train carry my sister, …
3 Same train, same train,
   Same train a blowin' at de station,
   Same train, same train,
   Same train blowin' at de station, …

(Johnson and Johnson 1926, 60)

Prayer Focus: When death comes creeping in my room, I'm going to ride to my home in glory on the same train that has carried so many courageous African American heroes home.

BIOY: Amos 6-9 (273/92)

Psalm 107
"Satan's Camp a-Fire"

FIER, my Saviour, fier,
Satan's camp a-fire;
Fier, believer, fier,
Satan's camp a-fire.

(Allen, Ware, and Garrison 1867, 27)

Prayer Focus: Jesus can fix it! Jesus can fix it! Jesus can fix it! Jesus can fix it! Jesus can fix it! Jesus can fix it! Jesus can fix it! Jesus can fix it! Jesus can fix it! Jesus can fix it! Jesus can fix it! Jesus can fix it!

Jesus fixed it for my mother! Jesus fixed it for my father! Jesus fixed it for my sister! Jesus fixed it for my brother! Jesus fixed it for the preacher! Jesus fixed it for the deacon! Jesus can fix it for me! Jesus will fix it after awhile! You can't hurry God.

Work it out, Lord! I give thanks to you for your goodness and for working it out for me.

BIOY: Obadiah 1 (274/91)

John 1-2
"Scandalize My Name"

1   WELL, I met my sister de other day,
    Give her my right han',
    Jes' as soon as ever my back was turned
    she took 'n' scandalize' my name.
    Do you call dat a sister?
    No! No! you call dat a sister?
    No! No! you call dat a sister?
    No! No! scandalize' my name.

2   Well, I met my brother de other day, ...
    him ... he ... brother? ...

3   Well, I met my preacher de other day, ...
    him/her ... he/she ... 'ligion? ...

(Songs of Zion 1981, 159)

Prayer Focus: Lord, I been 'buked, scorned, and talked about as sure as you're born. I'm glad you care for me. I am your child. I am somebody! Lord, I will respect myself and carry myself with, "R-E-S-P-E-C-T!"

BIOY: Jonah 1-4 (275/90)

∙◎∙◎∙◎∙◎∙◎∙◎∙◎∙◎∙◎∙◎∙◎∙◎∙◎∙◎∙◎∙◎∙

Psalm 108
"Shall I Die?"

1   BELIEVER, O shall I die?
    O my army, shall I die?
2   Jesus die, shall I die?
    Die on the cross, shall I die?
3   Die, die, die, shall I die?
    Jesus da coming, shall I die?
4   Run for to meet him, shall I die?
    Weep like a weeper, shall I die?
5   Mourn like a mourner, shall I die?
    Cry like a crier, shall I die?

(Allen, Ware, and Garrison 1867, 41)

Prayer Focus: Trouble always in my way. Lord, you died for me; shall I die for you? Yes, die I shall! Oh, my God! Oh, Jesus. Be exalted, O God, above the heavens and your glory above all the earth! Deliver your beloved; trample down the satanic lynch mob coming after me.

BIOY: Micah 1-4 (276/89)

John 3-4
"Shine for Jesus"
(Matt. 5:16)

Chorus

    SHINE when trouble shake you;
    Shine, when friends forsake you;
    All the way, ev'ry day,
    There's a crown a-waiting;
    Shine, when foes assail you;
    Shine, when others fail you;
    Keep your eyes on Jesus,
    And shine, shine, shine.

(Boatner and Townsend 1927, 35)

Prayer Focus: Great God of providence, I heard the voice of Jesus say, "Come unto me and rest." Lord, I came to you as I was, weary, worn, and sad. I found in you a resting place and you have made me glad. Now Lord, send me a song to help me along this pilgrim's journey. Help me sing and pray every day. Let the Light from the Lighthouse shine on me and I'll let him shine in me and through me.

BIOY: Micah 5-7 (277/88)

Psalm 109
"Take Me to the Water"

1 TAKE me to the water (x3)
   to be baptized.
2 None but the righteous (x3)
   shall see God.
3 I love Jesus (x3)
   yes I do.
4 He's my Savior (x3)
   yes He is.

(Warren 1997, 91)

Prayer Focus: Help me, O Lord, my God! The mouths of the unrighteous have opened against me. They have spoken against me with a lying tongue, surrounded me with words of hatred, and fought against me without cause. They have rewarded my good with evil. They hate me because I'm different. They smile in my face and stab me in my back. Lord, you are my strength, shield, rock, and redeemer! In thee I trust.

BIOY: Nahum 1-3 (278/87)

John 5-6
"Shout On, Children"

1   SHOUT on, chil'en, you never die; *Glory hallelu!*
    You in de Lord, an' de Lord in you; *Glory hallelu!*
2   Shout an' pray both night an' day; ...
    How can you die, you in de Lord? ...
3   Come on, chil'en, let's go home; ...
    O I'm so glad you're in de Lord. ...

(Allen, Ware, and Garrison 1867, 60)

Prayer Focus: "God is Spirit, and those who worship Him must worship in spirit and truth" (John 4:24). "Most assuredly, I say to you, he who hears My word and believes in Him who sent Me has everlasting life, and shall not come into judgment, but has passed from death into life" (John 5:24). God Almighty, I honor your Son Jesus just as I honor you!

BIOY: Habakkuk 1-3 (279/86)

Psalm 110
"Singin' Wid a Sword in Ma Han'"

SINGIN' wid a sword in ma han', Lord,
Singin' wid a sword in ma han',
Singin' wid a sword in ma han', Lord,
Singin' wid a sword in ma han'.

1 *Purtiest* singin' ever I heard, *'Way ovah on de hill,*
De angels sing *an' I sing too,*
   Singin' *wid a sword in ma han', Lord,*
Singin' *wid a sword in ma han', Lord,*
   Singin' *wid a sword in ma han'.*

2 Purtiest shoutin' ever I heard, …
De angels shout an' I shout too, …
Purtiest preachin' ever I heard, …
De angels preach an' I preach'd too, …

3 Purtiest prayin' ever I heard, …
De angels pray an' I pray'd too, …

4 Purtiest mournin' ever I heard, …
De angels mourn an' I mourn'd too, …

(Johnson and Johnson 1925, 86)

Prayer Focus: Lord, you are my light and my salvation, my strength and song! (Ps. 27:1; 118:14).

BIOY: Zephaniah 1–3 (280/85)

John 7-8
"Sinner, Please Don't Let dis Harves' Pass"

SINNER, please don't let dis harves' pass,
dis harves' pass,
Sinner, please don't let dis harves' pass,
harves' pass,
Sinner, please don't let dis harves' pass,
An' die, an lose yo' soul at las' yo' soul at las'.

1 Sinner, O, see dat cruel tree, dat cruel tree, Lord!
   Sinner, O, see dat cruel tree, ...
   Sinner, O, see dat cruel tree,
   Where Christ has died for you an' me ....

2 I know dat my redeemer lives, ... (3x)
   Sinner, please don't let dis harves' pass....

3 O My God is a mighty man o' war, ... (3x)
   Sinner please don't let dis harves' pass....

(Johnson and Johnson 1926, 50)

Prayer Focus: "You shall know the truth and the truth shall make you free" (John 8:31–32; cf. 44–45). Lord, I was blind but now I see! Hallelujah!

BIOY: Haggai 1-2 (281/84)

Psalm 111
"Sinner, Won't Die no More"

O DE Lamb done been down here an' died,
De Lamb done been down here an' died,
O de Lamb done been down here an' died,
Sinner won't die no mo'.

1 I wonder what bright angels, angels, angels,
   I wonder what bright angels,
   De robes all ready now.

2 O see dem ships come a-sailing, sailing, sailing,
   O see dem ships come a-sailing,
   De robes all ready now.

(Allen, Ware, and Garrison 1867, 85)

Prayer Focus: Jesus, my Lord and Savior, Lamb of God, I do believe. You done been down here, died for my sins, and now live forevermore (Rev. 1:18).

BIOY: Zechariah 1–4 (282/83)

John 9-10
"Sit Down, Servant"

SIT down, servant, can't sit down;
Sit down, servant, can't sit down;
Sit down, servant, can't sit down;
Soul so happy, Lord, I can't sit down.

1   *That ain't all, you know, you promise me,*
               promise me,
   A long white robe and a starry crown;
   Go yonder, angel, get me a long white robe,
   Place it on my servant's frame,
      Now servant do sit down.

2   That ain't all, you know, you promise me,
               promise me,
   A starry crown and a pair of wings;
   Go yonder, angel, get me a pair of wings,
   Place them on my servant's frame,
      Now servant do sit down.

3   That ain't all, you know, you promise me,
               promise me,
   A pair of wings and a starry crown;
   Go yonder, angel, get me a starry crown,
   Place it on my servant's head,
      Now servant do sit down.

(Boatner and Townsend 1927, 20)

Prayer Focus: I am in your hand of protection!

BIOY: Zechariah 5-7 (283/82)

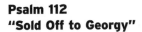

Psalm 112
"Sold Off to Georgy"

1   FAREWELL, fellow sarvants! O ho! O ho!
      I'm gwine way to leabe you; O ho! O ho!
      I'm gwine to leabe de ole county; O ho! O ho!
      I'm sold off to Georgy! O ho! O ho!

2   Farewell, ole plantation, (O ho! O ho!)
      Farewell, de ole quarter, (O ho! O ho!)
      Un daddy, un mammy, (O ho! O ho!)
      Un master, un missus! (O ho! O ho!)

3   My dear wife un one chile, (O ho! O ho!)
      My poor heart is breaking; (O ho! O ho!)
      No more shall I see you, (O ho! O ho!)
      Oh, no more foreber! (O ho! O ho!)

(Southern 1997, 157)

Prayer Focus: Lord, it's a terrible thing to be separated from family and friends against one's will. Lord, heal the pain.

BIOY: Zechariah 8–11 (284/81)

John 11-12
"Some O' These Days"

1   I'M goin'-t sit down at the welcome table,
    I'm goin'-t sit down at the welcome table,
    Some o' these days, (Hallelujah),
    I'm goin'-t sit down at the welcome table,
    I'm goin'-t sit down at the welcome table,
    Some o' these days.
2   I'm goin'-t feast on milk and honey, ...
3   I'm goin'-t sing and never get tired, ...
4   I'm goin'-t tell God all of my troubles, ...
5   I'm goin'-t tell God how you treat me, ...
6   God's goin'-t set this world on fire, ...
7   God's goin'-t stop that long-tongue liar, ...
             (The New National Baptist Hymnal 1977, 495)

Prayer Focus: If Jesus wept (John 11:35), then I do believe that when life's ups don't outweigh the downs then I, too, can fall on my knees with my face to the rising sun, and cry, "Oh, Lord, have mercy on me."

BIOY: Zechariah 12-14 (285/80)

Psalm 113
"Some Valiant Soldier" (Mark 15:21)

OH Lord, I want some valiant soldier,
I want some valiant soldier,
I want some valiant soldier,
To help me bear de cross.
For I weep, I weep,
I can't hold out;
If any mercy, Lord,
O pity poor me.

(Allen, Ware, and Garrison 1867, 50)

Prayer Focus: Lord, if you could not bear your cross without help, why do I keep thinking that I can bear my cross without help? I am not complaining—no cross, no crown. I am asking for help. Father, I stretch my hand to thee; no other help I know. Send help in any form, shape, or fashion. Please, Sir Jesus, have mercy. Help me hold out until my change comes.

BIOY: Malachi 1-4 (286/79)

John 13-14
"Somebody's Knockin' at Yo' Do'"
(Rev. 3:20)

SOMEBODY'S knockin' at yo' do'
Somebody's knockin' at yo' do'
O, sinner, why don't you answer?
Somebody's knockin' at yo' do'.

1   Knocks like Jesus,
    Somebody's knockin' at yo' do'
    Knocks like Jesus,
    Somebody's knockin' at yo' do'
    O, sinner, why don't you answer?
    Somebody's knockin' at yo' do'.

2   O, Answer Jesus,
    Somebody's knockin' at yo' do'
    Answer Jesus, ...

(Johnson and Johnson 1925, 85)

Prayer Focus: Somebody's knocking at my door? Is it you, Lord? Somebody's ringing my bell? Come in, Lord.

BIOY: Matthew 1-3 (287/78)

Psalm 114
"Sometimes I Feel Like a Moanin' Dove"

1   SOMETIMES I feel like a moanin' dove,
     Sometimes I feel like a moanin' dove,
     Sometimes I feel like a moanin' dove,
     A long ways, long ways,
     long ways from home,
     A long ways from home,
     long ways from home.
2   Sometimes I feel like a motherless chil',
     Sometimes I feel like a motherless chil',
     Sometimes I feel like a motherless chil',

(Songs of Zion 1981, 155)

Prayer Focus: When I think of home, I think of a resting place—a place where there is peace, quiet, and serenity. I long for a place where love is overflowing. Lord, I wish I was up there with you. I miss you. I love you. Oh God, living in this world is so hard! Mercy!

BIOY: Matthew 4-6 (288/77)

🔵🔵🔵🔵🔵🔵🔵🔵🔵🔵🔵🔵🔵🔵🔵🔵🔵🔵🔵🔵🔵🔵

John 15-16
"Sometimes I Feel Like a Motherless Child"

1   SOMETIMES I feel like a motherless child, (3x)
    A long ways from home; A long ways from home.
    True believer, A long ways from home,
    A long ways from home.
2   Sometimes I feel like I'm almos' gone, (3x)
    Way up in de heab'nly lan';
    Way up in de heab'nly lan'.
    True believer, way up in de heab'nly lan',
    Way up in the heab'nly lan'.
3   Sometimes I feel like a motherless child, (3x)
    A long ways from home.

(Johnson and Johnson 1926, 30)

Prayer Focus: Thank you for sending the Comforter.

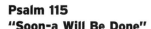

Psalm 115
"Soon-a Will Be Done"

SOON-A will be done
a-with the troubles of the world,
Troubles of the world,
The troubles of the world.
Soon-a will be done
a-with the troubles of the world,
Goin' home to live with God.

1   No more weeping and a-wailing, (3x)
    Goin' home to live with God.
2   I want t' meet my mother, (3x)
    Goin' home to live with God.
3   I want t' meet my Jesus, (3x)
    Goin' home to live with God.
             (The New National Baptist Hymnal 1977, 492)

Prayer Focus: Soon and very soon I'll be done with the cares of this world!

BIOY: Matthew 10-12 (290/75)

John 17-18
"Stan' Still Jordan"

STAN' still Jordan, Stan' still Jordan,
Stan' still Jordan, Lord I can't stan' still.

1 I got a mother in heaven,
   I got a mother in heaven,
   I got a mother in heaven,
   Lord I can't stan' still.

2 When I get up in glory, (3x)
   Lord I can't stan' still.

3 Jordan river, (3x)
   is chilly and cold.

4 It will chill-a my body, (3x)
   but not my soul.

(Johnson and Johnson 1925, 82)

Prayer Focus: "Sanctify them by Your truth. Your word is truth" (John 17:17). Make us one!

BIOY: Matthew 13-15 (291/74)

Psalm 116
"You Won't Find a Man Like Jesus"

LIKE Jesus, like Jesus;
And you won't find a man like Jesus,
Like Jesus, like Jesus.

1   You may search from sea to sea,
    But this thing is clear to me,
    That you won't find a man like Jesus.

2   You may search up in the air,
    But you will not find Him there,
    No, you won't find a man like Jesus.

3   You may search all under the ground,
    But I know He can't be found,
    No, you won't find a man like Jesus.

4   You may search from pole to pole,
    You may search all over the world,
    But you won't find a man like Jesus.

(Gospel Pearls 1921, 160)

Prayer Focus: I offer sacrifices of thanksgiving.

BIOY: Matthew 16-19 (292/73)

John 19-20
"Stars Begin to Fall"
(Matt. 24:29; Rev. 8:10)

1   I TINK I hear my brudder* say,
     Call de nation great and small;
     I lookee on de God's right hand,
     When de stars begin to fall.

2   Oh what a mournin' (sister),
     Oh what a mournin' (brudder),
     Oh, what a mournin',
     When de stars begin to fall.

(Allen, Ware, and Garrison 1867, 25)

* Titty Nelly, De member, &c.

Prayer Focus: Creator God, I have sinned and come short of your glory. I thank you that I have been justified freely by your grace through the redemption that is in Christ Jesus, whom you set forth as propitiation by his blood through faith.

BIOY: Matthew 20-22 (293/72)

Psalm 117
"Stay in the Field"

O STAY in the field, childer-en-ah,
Stay in the field, childer-en-ah.
Stay in the field,
Until the war is ended.

1   I've got my breastplate, sword and shield,
    Till the war is ended;
    And I'll go marching thro' the field,
    Till the war is ended.

2   Satan thought he had me fast, …
    But thank the Lord I'm free at last, …

(Southern 1997, 212)

Prayer Focus: I am a soldier of the cross, a follower of the Lamb! I must fight if I would reign, increase my courage, Lord! I'll bear the toil, and endure the pain, supported by thy Word.

BIOY: Matthew 23-25 (294/71)

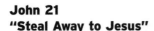

John 21
"Steal Away to Jesus"

STEAL away, steal away,
steal away to Jesus!
Steal away, steal away home,
I ain't got long to stay here.

1   My Lord, He calls me,
   He calls me by the thunder,
   The trumpet sounds within-a my soul,
   I ain't got long to stay here.

2   Green trees a-bending,
   po' sinner stand a-trembling, …

(Johnson and Johnson 1925, 114)

Prayer Focus: "Keep me as the apple of Your eye; Hide me under the shadow of Your wings, From the wicked who oppress me, From my deadly enemies who surround me" (Ps. 17:8–9).

BIOY: Matthew 26-28 (295/70)

Psalm 118
"Study War No More"
(Isa. 2:4; Micah 4:3)

1 GOING to lay down my sword and shield,
   Down by the riverside, Down by the riverside,
   Down by the riverside;
   Going to lay down my sword and shield,
   Down by the riverside,
   Going to study war no more.
   Ain't going-t' study war no more, (6x)
2 Going to lay down my burden, ...
3 Going to try on my starry crown, ...
4 Going to meet my dear old father, ...
5 Going to meet my dear old mother, ...
6 Going to meet my loving Jesus, ...
                    (The AME Zion Bicentennial Hymn 1996, 625)

Prayer Focus: I'm tired and weary but I must toil on.
Lord, this world suffers violence. I pray for the day
when the devil will be cast into the lake of fire. When the
battle is over, there'll be peace, and I shall wear a crown.

BIOY: Mark 1-4 (296/69)

Acts 1-2
"Surely He Died on Calvary"

CALVARY, Calvary, Calvary, (2x)
Surely He died on Calvary.

1   Ev'ry time I think about Jesus,
    Ev'ry time I think about Jesus,
    Ev'ry time I think about Jesus,
    Surely He died on Calvary.

2   Don't you hear the hammer ringing? ...

3   Don't you hear Him calling His Father? ...

4   Don't you hear Him say, "It is finished?" ...

5   Jesus furnished my salvation, ...

6   Sinner, do you love my Jesus? ...

(Boatner and Townsend 1927, 6)

Prayer Focus: Lord, they tortured and killed you. Wild lynch mobs tortured and killed innocent African Americans. You died that I may live again. They died that I may have courage to live free.

BIOY: Mark 5-7 (297/68)

Psalm 119:1-40
"Swing Low Sweet Chariot"
(2 Kings 2:11)

SWING low sweet chariot,
Comin' for to carry me home,
Swing low sweet chariot,
Comin' for to carry me home (repeat)

1   I look'd over Jordan, an' what did I see,
     Comin' for to carry me home,
     A band of angels comin' after me,
     Comin' for to carry me home.

2   If you get-a dere befo' I do,
     Comin' for to carry me home,
     Tell all my friends I'm comin' too,
     Comin' for to carry me home.

(Johnson and Johnson 1925, 62)

Prayer Focus: Open my eyes that I may see wondrous things from your Law. Turn my eyes away from worthless things. Teach me, revive me, in your way and righteousness, according to your Word.

BIOY: Mark 8-10 (298/67)

Acts 3-4
"Tell My Jesus"

1   IN de mornin' when I rise,
    Tell my Jesus huddy, oh;*
    I wash my hands in de mornin' glory,
    Tell my Jesus huddy, oh.

2   Mornin', Hester, mornin', gal,
    Tell my Jesus huddy, oh;
    I wash my hands in de mornin' glory,
    Tell my Jesus huddy, oh.

3   Say, brudder Sammy, you got de order, …

4   You got the order, and I got de order, …

(Allen, Ware, and Garrison 1867, 15)

  * Morning.

Prayer Focus: Just a closer walk with thee; grant it Jesus if you please. Daily walking close with thee—dear Lord, let it be. Hear thou the prayer I make on bended knee. Hear now my earnest plea. More love, O Christ to thee, more love to thee.

BIOY: Mark 11-13 (299/66)

Psalm 119:41-80
"The Day of Judgment"
(Acts 2:20; Rev. 6:12)

1   AND de moon will turn to blood,
    And de moon will turn to blood,
    And de moon will turn to blood,
    In dat day O yoy, * *my soul!*
    And de moon will turn to blood in dat day.
2   And you'll see de stars a-fallin', ...
3   And de world will be on fire, ...
4   And you'll hear de saints a-singin'; ...
5   And de Lord will say to de sheep, ...
6   For to go to Him right hand; ...
7   But de goats must go to de left, ...
                    (Allen, Ware, and Garrison 1867, 53)

* "A sort of prolonged wail."

Prayer Focus: Oh happy day, when Jesus washed my sins away! Glory to your name!

BIOY: Mark 14-16 (300/65)

Acts 5-6
"The Gold Band"

1 GWINE to march away in de gold band,
In de army, bye-and-bye;
Gwine to march away in de gold band,
In de army, bye-and-bye.
Sinner, what you gwine to do dat day?
Sinner, what you gwine to do dat day?
When de fire's a rolling behind you,
In de army, bye-and-bye.
2 Sister Mary gwine to hand down the robe,
In de army, bye-and-bye;
Gwine to hand down the robe and the gold band,
In de army, bye-and-bye.

(Allen, Ware, and Garrison 1867, 83)

Prayer Focus: Lord, I got heaven on my mind. The devil can't stop me; his demons can't block me. I'm going to do right and shun wrong. I'm going to obey you, O God (Acts 5:29). You alone I trust.

BIOY: Luke 1-4 (301/64)

DAY 302

Psalm 119:81-120
"The Golden Altar"
(Rev. 7:9)

JOHN saw-r-O, John saw-r-O,
John saw de holy number
settin' on de golden altar!
1   It's a little while longer yere below,
    yere below, yere below,
    It's a little while longer yere below,
    Before de Lamb of God!
2   And home to Jesus we will go,
    we will go, we will go,
    And home to Jesus we will go,
    We are de people of de Lord.
3   Dere's a golden slipper in de heavens for you, …
    Before de Lamb of God….
4   I wish I'd been dere when prayer begun, …
5   To see my Jesus about my sins, …
6   Then home to glory we will go, …
                (Allen, Ware, and Garrison 1867, 77)

Prayer Focus: Lord, I got heaven on my mind.

BIOY: Luke 5-7 (302/63)

Acts 7-8
"The Good Old Way"

1 AS I went down in de valley to pray,
  Studying about dat good old way,
  When you shall wear de starry crown,
  Good Lord, show me de way.

2 O mourner,* let's go down, let's go down,
  O mourner, let's go down,
  Down in de valley to pray.

(Allen, Ware, and Garrison 1867, 84)

* Sister, etc.

Prayer Focus: Lord, I'm down and out in the valley of a sin-filled life. The preacher says there is a Lily in this valley, bright as the morning star, a Lily more beautiful than the Rose of Sharon, a Lily sweeter than honey in the honeycomb. I pray that I find this Lily. You the Lily? Thank God you found me!

BIOY: Luke 8-11 (303/62)

DAY 304

Psalm 119:121-176
"The Graveyard"
(Brudder Sammy)

1   WHO gwine to lay dis body,
    Member, O, shout glory. *
    And-a who gwine to lay dis body,
    Oh, ring Jerusalem.
2   O call all de member to de graveyard, ...
3   O graveyard, ought to know me, ...
4   O grass grow in de graveyard, ...
5   O I reel† and I rock in de graveyard, ...

(Allen, Ware, and Garrison 1867, 15)

  * Sing glory, Graveyard.
  † Shout, Wheel.

Prayer Focus: Though I am persecuted without a cause, my heart stands in awe of your Word. I rejoice at your Word as one who finds great treasure (Ps. 119:161–162). Direct my steps by your Word (Ps. 119:133).

BIOY: Luke 12-14 (304/61)

Acts 9-10
"The Heaven Bells"

1   O MOTHER I believe, O mother I believe,
    O mother I believe, That Christ was crucified!
2   O don't you hear the Heaven bells
        a-ringing over me?
    a-ringing over me? a-ringing over me?
    O don't you hear the Heaven bells
        a-ringing over me?
    It sounds like the judgment day!
                    (Allen, Ware, and Garrison 1867, 79)

Prayer Focus: Lord, when I start going crooked, put me on a street called Straight that I may inquire at thy house of prayer about godly wisdom, instruction, and gain a heart of understanding.

BIOY: Luke 15-17 (305/60)

Psalm 120
"The Hypocrite and the Concubine"

1   HYPOCRITE and the concubine,
     Livin' among the swine,
     They run to God with the lips and tongue,
     And leave all the heart behind.
     Aunty, did you hear when Jesus rose?
     Did you hear when Jesus rose?
     Aunty, did you hear when Jesus rose?
     He rose and he 'scend on high.

                        (Allen, Ware, and Garrison 1867, 70)

Prayer Focus: Deliver my soul, O Lord, from lying lips and those who hate peace. I am for peace, but when I speak, they are for war. Anoint me as a minister of reconciliation. Racial hatred, cultural intolerance, and discrimination of all kinds is wrong. Let the power of the Holy Ghost fall on me, fall fresh on me. Empower me to do thy will.

BIOY: Luke 18-21 306/59

Acts 11-12
"The Lonesome Valley"

MY brudder,*want to get religion?
Go down in de lonesome valley,
My brudder, want to get religion?
Go down in de lonesome valley.

1   Go down in de lonesome valley,
    Go down in de lonesome valley, my Lord;
    Go down in de lonesome valley,
    To meet my Jesus dere.
2   O feed on milk and honey, ...
3   O John he write de letter, ...
4   And Mary and Marta read 'em, ...
                    (Allen, Ware, and Garrison 1867, 5)

* Sister Katy, etc.

Prayer Focus: Help me to be courageous enough to go down the lonesome valley, even to be martyred.

BIOY: Luke 22-24 (307/58)

Psalm 121
"The Old Ship of Zion"

1 WHAT ship is that you're enlisted upon?
O glory hallelujah!
'Tis the old ship of Zion, hallelujah! (2x)

2 And who is the Captain
of the ship that you're on? …
My Saviour is the Captain, hallelujah! (2x)

North Carolina Version

1 Don't you see that ship, a-sailin',
a-sailin', a-sailin',
Don't you see that ship a-sailin',
Gwine over to the Promised Land?
I asked my Lord, shall I ever be the one, (3x)
To go sailin', sailin', sailin', sailin',
Gwine over to the Promised Land?

2 She sails like she is heavy loaded, …

3 King Jesus is the Captain, …

4 The Holy Ghost is the Pilot, …

(Allen, Ware, and Garrison 1867, 102)

Prayer Focus: Lord, I got my ticket. When can I go?

BIOY: John 1–3 (308/57)

Acts 13-14
"The Resurrection Morn"

1   O RUN, Mary, run, *Hallelu, hallelu!*
    O run, Mary, run *Hallelujah!*
2   It was early in de mornin', …
3   That she went to de sepulchre, …
4   And de Lord he wasn't da, …
5   But she see a man a-comin', …
6   And she thought it was de gardender, …
7   But he say, "O touch me not, …
8   "For I am not yet ascended, …
9   "But tell to my disciples, …
10   "Dat de Lord he is arisen." …
11   So run, Mary, run …

(Allen, Ware, and Garrison 1867, 54)

Prayer Focus: You arose! You arose! You arose from the dead and you shall bear my spirit home!

BIOY: John 4-6 (309/56)

Psalm 122
"The Sin-Sick Soul"

BRUDDER George is a-gwine to glory,
Take car' de sin-sick soul,
Brudder George is a-gwine to glory,
Take car' de sin-sick soul,
Brudder George is a-gwine to glory,
Take car' de sin-sick soul.

(Allen, Ware, and Garrison 1867, 49)

Prayer Focus: Lord, I am glad when they say, "Let us go into the house of the Lord" (Ps. 122:1). I lift up my eyes and see the stars. I hear the rolling thunder. Thy power throughout the universe is displayed. Lord, my help does not come from the hills, from idols made by human hands, or from the creatures you have made. My help comes from you! You are my all and all. To choose to worship another that cannot see, cannot hear, and to whom I cannot speak would be foolish. You alone have all power and wisdom. You are my God— righteous and full of compassion!

BIOY: John 7-9 (310/55)

Acts 15-16
"The Social Band"

1 BRIGHT angels on the water,
  Hovering by the light;
  Poor sinner stand in the darkness,
  And cannot see the light.

2 I want Aunty Mary* for to go with me,
  I want Aunty Mary for to go with me,
  I want Aunty Mary for to go with me,
  To join the social band.

(Allen, Ware, and Garrison 1867, 105)

* Brother David.

Prayer Focus: At midnight Paul and Silas were praying and singing hymns to you, O God, as the other prisoners listened. Lord, may I also in my midnight experiences boldly pray and sing hymns to you as listeners witness your deliverance power!

BIOY: John 10-12 (311/54)

Psalm 123
"The Sweets of Liberty"

1   IS there a man that never sighed
      to set the prisoner free?
    Is there a man that never prized
      the sweets of liberty?
    Then let him, let him breathe unseen
      or in a dungeon lie.
    Nor never, never know the sweets
      that liberty can give.

2   Is there a heart so cold in Man
      Can galling fetters crave?
    Is there a wretch so truly low,
      Can stoop to be a slave?
    O, let him, then, in chains be bound,
      In chains and bondage live; …

3   Is there a breast so chilled in life,
      Can nurse the coward's sigh?
    Is there a creature so debased,
      Would not for freedom die?
    O, let him, then, be doomed to crawl,
      Where only reptiles live; …

(Southern 1997, 141)

Prayer Focus: Increase my love for my neighbor, and even for my enemies.

BIOY: John 13-16 (312/53)

Acts 17-18
"The Time Ain't Long"

1 OH, the time ain't long,
 Oh, the time ain't long,
 Oh, the time ain't long,
 Oh, the time ain't long, (ain't long.)

2 There's a Star in the east,
 There's a Star in the west,
 An' I wish that Star,
 Was in my breast, (my breast.)

3 I've got my hand,
 On the gospel plow,
 Well, I'm bound to reach
 My Father's house, (His house.)

4 I'm on my way,
 Up the gospel track,
 Yes, I'm on my way,
 An' I won't turn back, (turn back.)

(Boatner and Townsend 1927, 7)

Prayer Focus: I still got heaven on my mind.

BIOY: John 17-19 (313/52)

Psalm 124
"The Time for Praying"

1 THE time for praying won't be long,
   The time for praying won't be long,
   The time for praying won't be long,
   Go, shepherd, feed my sheep.
2 The time for singing won't be long,
   The time for singing won't be long,
   The time for singing won't be long,
   Go, shepherd, feed my sheep.
3 Hum —
   Hum —
   Hum —
   Go, shepherd, feed my sheep.

(Songs of Zion 1981, 133)

Prayer Focus: Lord, the harvest is plentiful, but the laborers few (Matt. 9:37). Help me grow in spiritual maturity and good works so that the works I do may speak for me. I don't want to labor in vain.

BIOY: John 20-21 (314/51)

Acts 19–20
"The Trouble of the World"

1 I WANT to be* my Fader's chil'en,
    I want to be my Fader's chil'en,
    I want to be my Fader's chil'en,
    Roll, Jordan, roll.
    O say,† ain't you done wid de trouble ob de world,
    Ah! trouble ob de world, Ah!
    Say ain't you done wid de trouble ob de world,
    Ah Roll, Jordan, roll.

2 I ask de Lord how long I hold 'em, (ter)
    Hold 'em to de end.

3 My sins so heavy I can't get along, Ah! &c.

4 I cast my sins in de middle of de sea, Ah! &c.

                  (Allen, Ware, and Garrison 1867, 8)

  * O you ought to be.
  † My sister, My mudder, etc.

Prayer Focus: Lord, soon and very soon, I will be done with the troubles of this world. Hallelujah!

BIOY: Acts 1–4 (315/50)

Psalm 125
"The White Marble Stone"

1   SISTER Dolly* light the lamp,
    and the lamp light the road,
    And I wish I been there
    for yed-de Jordan roll.
2   O the city light the lamp,
    the white man he will sold,
    And I wish I been there, etc.
3   O the white marble stone,
    and the white marble stone, etc.

(Allen, Ware, and Garrison 1867, 42)

* Believer, Patty, etc.

Prayer Focus: If it had not been for you, Lord, on our side, where would we be (Ps. 124:1)? My help is in you. In you, O Lord, I put my trust. Those who trust in you shall be like Mount Zion, which cannot be moved, but abides forever (Ps. 125:1).

BIOY: Acts 5-8 (316/49)

Acts 21-22
"The Winter"

O DE vinter, O de vinter,
   O de vinter'll soon be ober,* chilen, (3x)
Yes, my Lord!
1 'Tis Paul and Silas bound in chains, chains,
   And one did weep,†
   and de oder one did pray, oder one did pray!
2 You bend your knees‡ on holy ground, ground,
   And ask de Lord, Lord, for to turn you around,
   For de vinter, etc.
3 I turn my eyes towards the sky, sky,
   And ask de Lord, Lord, for wings to fly.
4 For you see me gwine 'long so, so,
   I has my tri-trials yer below.

(Allen, Ware, and Garrison 1867, 78)

   * Am a-comin'
   † Sing
   ‡ I bend my knees, etc.

Prayer Focus: Creator of all the earth, turn my winter into spring.

BIOY: Acts 9-11 (317/48)

DAY 318

Psalm 126
"There is a Light Shining"

1 THERE is a light shining in the heavens for me,
  There is a light shining for me.
  Oh, *'way over yonder*
  in that ever bright world,
  There is a light shining for me.
2 Oh, I have to pray so hard, so hard,
  I have to pray so hard. But, …
3 My lonesome way so dark, so dark,
  My lonesome way so dark. But, …

(Boatner and Townsend 1927, 63)

Prayer Focus: I shall come rejoicing, bringing in the sheaves. You are my joy in the midst of sorrow.

BIOY: Acts 12-14 (318/47)

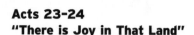

Acts 23-24
"There is Joy in That Land"

1   THERE is *Joy* in that land,
    There is *Joy* in that land,
    There is *Joy* in that land
    where I'm bound, where I'm bound;
    There is *Joy* in that land,
    There is *Joy* in that land,
    There is *Joy* in that land,
    where I'm bound.

2   There is *Peace* in that land, …

3   There is *Love* in that land, …

(Boatner and Townsend 1927, 11)

Prayer Focus: Lord, I am bound for Canaan land, where there is joy, peace, and love. All along my pilgrim journey, Savior, let me walk with thee. Each day with you, Jesus, is sweeter than the day before. The best will be when I reach heaven's door.

BIOY: Acts 15-16 (319/46)

Psalm 127
"There's a Great Camp Meeting"

1   OH, walk together, children, *Don't you get weary,*
     Walk together, children, *Don't you get weary,*
     Walk together, children, *Don't you get weary,*
     There's a great camp meeting
       in the Promised Land.
2   Oh, talk together, children, …
3   Oh, sing together, children, …
4   Oh, get you ready, children, …
5   For Jesus is a-coming, …
6   Oh, I feel the spirit moving, …
7   Oh, now I'm getting happy, …

1,2   (Leader) Going to mourn and never tire, (3x)
      (Response) There's a great camp meeting
        in the Promised Land.
3   Going to sing, and never tire, (3x) …
4,5   Going to pray, and never tire, (3x) …
6,7   Going to shout, and never tire, (3x) …
        (The AME Zion Bicentennial Hymnal 1996, 616)

Prayer Focus: I am bound for the Promised Land!

BIOY: Acts 17-19 (320/45)

Acts 25-26
"There's a Little Wheel a-Turning"

1 THERE'S a lit'l wheel a-turnin' *in-a my heart,*
  There's a lit'l wheel a-turnin' *in-a my heart,*
  In-a my heart, In-a my heart,
  There's a lit'l wheel a-turnin'
  in-a my heart, in-a my heart.
2 O I feel so very happy, ...
3 O I feel like shouting, ...
4 There's a lit'l wheel a-turnin', ...
        (The AME Zion Bicentennial Hymnal 1996, 604)

Prayer Focus: Lord, in my heart there is a melody of love divine. Out of the depths of my heart I cry, "Jesus draw nigh, Jesus draw nigh." Lord, not only draw nigh, but draw me nearer, nearer, blessed Lord, to the cross where thou hast died.

BIOY: Acts 20-23 (321/44)

Psalm 128
"There's a Meeting Here Tonight"

1   I TAKE my text in Mattew,
and by de Revelation,
I know you by your garment,
Dere's a meeting here tonight.
Dere's a meeting here tonight, (Brudder Tony,)
Dere's a meeting here tonight, (Sister Rina,)
Dere's a meeting here tonight,
I hope to meet again.

2   Brudder John was a writer,
he write de laws of God;
Sister Mary say to brudder John,
"Brudder John, don't write no more."

(Allen, Ware, and Garrison 1867, 9)

Prayer Focus: Lord of all creation, all to Jesus I surrender.

BIOY: Acts 24-26 (322/43)

◉◎◉◎◉◎◉◎◉◎◉◎◉◎◉◎◉◎◉◎◉◎◉◎◉◎◉◎◉◎◉◎◉

Acts 27-28
"These Are all My Father's Children"

1   DESE all my fader's children,
    Dese all my fader's children,
    Dese all my fader's children,
    Outshine de sun.

2   My fader's done wid de trouble o' de world,
    wid de trouble o' de world,
    wid de trouble o' de world,
    My fader's done wid de trouble o' de world,
    Outshine de sun.

(Allen, Ware, and Garrison 1867, 101)

[**NOTE:** This is interesting as being probably the original of "Trouble of the World" (Day 315) and peculiarly so from the following custom, which is described by a North Carolina negro as existing in South Carolina. When a pater-familias dies, his family assemble(s) in the room where the coffin is, and, ranging themselves round the body in the order of age and relationship, sing this hymn, marching round and round. They also take the youngest and pass him first over and then under the coffin. Then two men take the coffin on their shoulders and carry it on the run to the grave.]

Prayer Focus: Father, you love us one and all. One day, I, too, will be done with the trouble of the world.

BIOY: Acts 27-28 (323/42)

Psalm 129
"This is the Trouble of the World"

I AX Fader Georgy for religion,
Fader Georgy wouldn't give me religion;
You give me religion for to run to my elder;
O dis is de trouble of de world.
Dis is de trouble of de world,
O,* Dis is de trouble of de world.

(Allen, Ware, and Garrison 1867, 99)

* (What you doubt for?) or
(What you shame for?) or
(take it easy) or (Tity 'Melia)

Prayer Focus: Enslaved African Americans were not allowed to have church (Berlin et al., 1998, 296). Lord, I speak against the religious persecution today of Christians around the world. Thy Kingdom come. Jesus, you are the answer for the world today.

BIOY: Romans 1-4 (324/41)

DAY 325

Revelation 1
"This Little Light of Mine"

1 THIS little light of mine, *I'm goin'a let it shine,*
   this little light of mine, *I'm goin'a let it shine;*
   this little light of mine, *I'm goin' a let it shine,*
   let it shine, let it shine, let it shine.
2 Everywhere I go, ...
3 All through the night, ...
                    (The AME Zion Bicentennial Hymnal 1996, 617)

Prayer Focus: I saw the light: no more darkness, no more night, no more pain, misery, or strife. I got to praise you, Lord, and let your light shine in me and through me everywhere I go. How I know my Savior lives! I feel you in my soul. You were dead; behold, you live forevermore! Hallelujah!

BIOY: Romans 5-8 (325/40)

Psalm 130
"'Tis the Old Ship of Zion"

'TIS the old ship of Zion,
'tis the old ship of Zion,
'tis the old ship of Zion,
get on board,
get on board.

1   It has landed many a thousand,
    it has landed many a thousand,
    it has landed many a thousand,
    get on board,
    get on board.

2   Ain't no danger in the water, …

3   It was good for my dear mother, …

4   It was good for my dear father, …

5   It will take us all to heaven, …

(The AME Zion Bicentennial Hymnal 1996, 612)

Prayer Focus: Out of the depths I cry to you. Jesus, draw closer to me. 'Tis so sweet to trust in you and to depend upon your Word. Lead me, guide me.

BIOY: Romans 9-12 (326/39)

Revelation 2-3
"To See God's Bleedin' Lam'"

WANT to go to heab'n, when I die,
when I die, when I die;
Want to go to heab'n, when I die,
To see God's bleedin' Lam'.

1   Jacob's ladder deep an' long,
    deep an' long, deep an' long;
    Jacob's ladder deep an' long,
    To see God's bleedin' Lam'.

2   See God's angel comin' down,
    comin' down, comin' down;
    See God's angel comin' down, ...

3   Comin' down in a sheet of blood,
    sheet of blood, sheet of blood;
    Comin' down in a sheet of blood, ...

4   Sheet of blood all mingled wid fire,
    mingled wid fire, mingled wid fire;
    Sheet of blood all mingled wid fire, ...

(Johnson and Johnson 1926, 152)

Prayer Focus: I want to see heaven, just like John.

BIOY: Romans 13-16 (327/38)

Psalm 131
"Too Late"

1   TOO late, too late, sinnah, Hm—too late;
Too late, too late, sinnah,
Carry de key an' gone home.
Massa Jesus lock de do' O, Lord! too late;
Massa Jesus lock de do',
Carry de key an' gone home.
Lock de do' an' take de key, O Lord! too late;
Carry de key an' gone home.

2   Too late, too late, false pretender, Hm—too late;
Too late, too late, backslider,
Carry de key an' gone home.

(Johnson and Johnson 1926, 102)

Prayer Focus: It's getting late, but it's not too late, to call on Jesus. Your blood still runs warm and covers a multitude of sins.

BIOY: 1 Corinthians 1–4 (328/37)

Revelation 4-5
"Trampin'"

*I'M trampin', trampin', Try'n' to make
 Heaven ma home.
I'm trampin', trampin', Try'n' to make
 Heaven ma home.
Hallelujah, I'm a-trampin', trampin',
 Try'n' to make Heaven ma home.
I'm trampin', trampin', Try'n' to make
 Heaven ma home.*

1 I've never been to Heaven but I've been tol'.
  Try'n' to make Heaven ma home.
  Dat de streets up dere are paved wid gol'.
  Try'n' to make Heaven ma home.
2 If you git dere befo' I do, …
  Tell all ma friends I'm coming too, …

(Songs of Zion 1981, 111)

Prayer Focus: I'm pressing on the upward way. Lord, I'm determined to make heaven my home and see that emerald like rainbow around your throne!

BIOY: 1 Corinthians 5-6 (329/36)

Psalm 132
"Travel On"

SISTER Rosy, you get to heaven before I go,
Sister, you look out for me,
I'm on de way.
Trabel on, trabel on,
you heaven born* soldier,
Trabel on, trabel on,
Go hear de what my Jesus say.

(Allen, Ware, and Garrison 1867, 31)

* Heaven-bound.

Prayer Focus: I'm tired and weary, but I must toil on. Lord, you have made us all one family through the blood of Adam (Acts 17:26). Many of my family and loved ones have made it to heaven before me, but I'll make it home some day. When we all get to heaven what a day of rejoicing that will be! When we all see Jesus, we'll shout and tell the story of how we made it over! It will be all right after awhile.

BIOY: 1 Corinthians 7-9 (330/35)

Revelation 6
"Trying to Get Home"

1   LORD, I'm bearin' heavy burdens,
     Tryin' to get home;
   Lord, I'm bearin' heavy burdens,
     Tryin' to get home;
   Lord, I'm bearin' heavy burdens,
   Lord, I'm bearin' heavy burdens,
   Lord, I'm bearin' heavy burdens,
     Tryin' to get home.

2   Lord, I'm climbin' high mountains, ...

3   Lord, I'm standin' hard trials, ...

(Songs of Zion 1981, 130)

Prayer Focus: I am often tossed and driven on this restless sea of time. Somber skies and howling tempests often hide the bright sunshine. Lord, I often wonder what makes my race so hard to run. Then I remember that the gospel message was not built on a platform of ease. More strength and courage please.

BIOY: 1 Corinthians 10-12 (331/34)

Psalm 133
"Turn, Sinner, Turn O!"

1   TURN, sinner, turn today,
    Turn, sinner, turn O!
    Turn, sinner, turn today,
    Turn, sinner, turn O!
2   Turn, O sinner, de worl' da gwine, …
3   Wait not for tomorrow's sun, …
4   Tomorrow's sun will sure to shine, …
5   The sun may shine, but on your grave, …
6   Hark! I hear dem sinner say, …
7   If you get to heaven I'll get there too, …
8   O sinner, you make mistake, …
9   While de lamp hold out to burn, …
10 De wile' sinner may return, …

          (Allen, Ware, and Garrison 1867, 36)

Prayer Focus: Lord, how good and pleasant it is to dwell in unity! You author peace, not confusion. May all things be done decently and in order.

BIOY: 1 Corinthians 13–16 (332/33)

Revelation 7
"Until I Reach-a Ma Home"

UNTIL I reach-a ma home,
Until I reach-a ma home,
I nevah inten' to give de journey ovah,
until I reach ma home. (True Believer ...)

1   O some say gim-me silvah,
    an' some say gim-me gol',
    But I say gim-me Jesus
    mos' precious to ma soul.

2   Dey say dat John de Baptis'
    was nothin' but a Jew,
    But de holy Bible tells us,
    Dat he was a preacher too.

(Johnson and Johnson 1925, 177)

Prayer Focus: I'm going to my Master's house. I'm not gonna let nobody turn me 'round! I got to keep on walking, and keep on marching, moving up the King's highway! He'll wipe away every tear. Glory!

BIOY: 2 Corinthians 1-3 (333/32)

Psalm 134
"Up on de Mountain"

1   WAY up on de mountain, Lord!
    Mountain top, Lord!
    I heard God talkin' Lord!
    Chillun, de chariot stop Lord!

2   One day Lord, one day Lord,
    Walkin' 'long Lord!
    Wid hung down head Lord!
    Chillun, an achin' heart Lord!

(Johnson and Johnson 1925, 64)

Prayer Focus: Hallelujah! I will lift up my hands in the house of the Lord and bless your holy name! Lord, I present my body to you as a living sacrifice. Wash me, cleanse me, and transform me. Renew my mind. Make me holy and acceptable. Make my body your sanctuary that I may be in your presence at all times and that you may be glorified in my life.

BIOY: 2 Corinthians 4-7 (334/31)

Revelation 8
"Wai', Mr. Mackright"

WAI', Mister Mackright,
an' 'e yed-de what Satan say:
Satan full me full of music,
an' tell me not to pray.
Mister Mackright cry holy;
O Lord, cry holy.

(Allen, Ware, and Garrison 1867, 43)

Prayer Focus: Lord, Satan is just like that old snake in the grass—always trying to bite me as I pass. This I know and know it well, he's doomed for trouble in a place called hell. He talks real big, but he's smaller than you. What he says isn't right. He's lost this fight! I'm going to serve you with all my might. Give me strength to fight the good fight. Eternal God, I magnify you. I praise your holy name! By your power and your authority, in the name of Jesus, I claim victory! Victory today is mine!

BIOY: 2 Corinthians 8-10 (335/30)

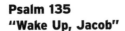

Psalm 135
"Wake Up, Jacob"

WAKE up, Jacob, day is a-breaking,
I'm on my way;
O, wake up, Jacob, day is a-breaking,
I'm on my way.

1 I want to go to heaven when I die,
   Do love de Lord!
   I want to go to heaven when I die,
   Do love de Lord!

2 Got some friends on de oder shore, ...
   I want to see 'em more an' more, ...

(Allen, Ware, and Garrison 1867, 65)

Prayer Focus: Lord, after I've walked in the pathway of duty and worked to the close of the day, I want to see you in your beauty, after I've gone the last mile of the way. I love you. I think about you all the day, my Buddy, my Friend.

BIOY: 2 Corinthians 11-13 (336/29)

Revelation 9
"Walk in Jerusalem Jus' Like John"
(I Want to Be Ready)
(Rev. 21:9-23)

I WANT to be ready,
I want to be ready,
want to be ready,
to walk in Jerusalem jus' like John.

1   John said de city was jus' foursquare,
    Walk in Jerusalem jus' like John,
    An' he declared he'd meet me dere;
    Walk in Jerusalem jus' like John.

2   Oh, John! Oh, John! what do you say? ...
    I'll be dere in de comin' day, ...

3   When Peter was preachin' at Pentacost, ...
    John, He was endowed wid de Holy Ghost, ...

(Johnson and Johnson 1926, 58)

Prayer Focus: John wrote there are twelve gates to the city and the streets are paved with gold (Rev. 21). I can't wait to walk in the New Jerusalem.

BIOY: Galatians 1-4 (337/28)

Psalm 136
"Walk With Me"

I WANT Jesus to walk with me,
I want Jesus to walk with me,
All along my pilgrim journey,
I want Jesus to walk with me.

1   In my trials, walk with me, (2x)
    When the shades of life are falling, Lord,
    I want Jesus to walk with me.

2   In my sorrows, walk with me, (2x)
    When my heart within is aching, Lord,
    I want Jesus to walk with me.

3   In my troubles, walk with me, (2x)
    When my life becomes a burden Lord,
    I want Jesus to walk with me.

(Boatner and Townsend 1927, 40)

Prayer Focus: Lord, I can't make it by myself. Walk with me, Lord. Stay by my side as I go down this road of life.

BIOY: Galatians 5-6 (338/27)

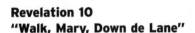

Revelation 10
"Walk, Mary, Down de Lane"

1   THREE long nights, an' three long days,
Jesus walkin' down de lane.
Three long nights, an' three long days,
Jesus walkin' down de lane.

2   In de mornin' down de lane, (4x)
Walk, Mary, down de lane,
   Walk, Mary, down de lane,
Walk, Mary, down de lane,
   Walk, Mary, down de lane.

3   Jesus calls you, down de lane, (4x)

4   In de heab'n, down de lane, (4x)

5   (I'm) 'fraid nobody, down de lane, (4x)

(Johnson and Johnson 1926, 147)

Prayer Focus: Give me strength and endurance to walk with confidence and courage in the face of pain, misery and strife. You alone will I trust and obey.

BIOY: Ephesians 1–3 (339/26)

Psalm 137
"Wayfaring Stranger"

1   I'M just a poor wayfaring stranger
    while journeying through this Land of woe
    But there's no sickness toil or danger
    In that bright world to which I go.
    I'm going there to see my Mother*
    she said she'd meet me when I would come
    I'm just a-going over Jordan
    I'm just a-going over home.

2   I know dark clouds will gather o'er me
    I know my way lies rough and steep
    But Beauteous Fields lie just before me
    Where gods redeemed their vigils keep.
           (*The AME Zion Bicentennial Hymnal 1996, 608*)

* Father … he … he'd. …

Prayer Focus: From the river banks of Babylon our tears of sorrow give us hope for tomorrow. Glory!

BIOY: Ephesians 4-6 (340/25)

Revelation 11
"We Am Clim'in Jacob's Ladder"
(Gen. 28:10-19)

1 WE am clim'in' Jacob's ladder,
   We am clim'in' Jacob's ladder,
   We am clim'in' Jacob's ladder,
   Soldiers of de cross.

2 Ev'ry roun' goes higher, higher,
   Ev'ry roun' goes higher, higher,
   Ev'ry roun' goes higher, higher,
   Soldiers of de cross.

(Johnson and Johnson 1925, 59)

Prayer Focus: Come, we that love the Lord, and let our joys be known. Join in a song with sweet accord. Join in a song with sweet accord. And thus surround the throne, and thus surround the throne. Lord, we're marching to Zion, beautiful, beautiful Zion. We're marching upward to Zion to the beautiful city of God! Glory! Hallelujah!

BIOY: Philippians 1-4 (341/24)

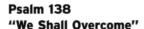

Psalm 138
"We Shall Overcome"

1 WE shall overcome, we shall overcome,
  we shall overcome *someday!*
  Oh, deep in my heart I do believe
  we shall overcome *someday!*
2 We'll walk hand in hand, ...
3 We shall all be free, ...
4 We shall live in peace, ...
5 The Lord will see us through, ...
      (The AME Zion Bicentennial Hymnal 1996, 640)

Prayer Focus: O Lord, I praise you with my whole heart. Though you sit high and lifted up, you regard the lowly. Though I walk in the midst of trouble, you will revive me. Stretch out your hand against my enemies and save me! This I do believe!

BIOY: Colossians 1-4 (342/23)

Revelation 12
"We Shall Walk Through the Valley"

WE shall walk thro' the valley
and the shadow of death,
We shall walk thro' the valley in peace:
For Jesus Himself will be our Leader,
We shall walk thro' the valley in peace.

1   There will be no sorrow there,
    There will be no sorrow there,
    For Jesus Himself will be our Leader,
    We shall walk thro' the valley in peace.

2   We shall meet our loved ones there,
    We shall meet our loved ones there, ...

3   We shall meet our Savior there, (2x) ...

4   He will wipe away ev'ry tear, (2x) ...

(Boatner and Townsend 1927, 55)

Prayer Focus: The devil has come down to the earth with great wrath; for he knows his time is short. But we have over come by the blood of the Lamb!

BIOY: 1 Thessalonians 1-2 (343/22)

Psalm 139
"We Will March Thro' the Valley"

1   WE will march thro' the valley in peace,
    We will march thro' the valley in peace;
    If Jesus himself be our leader,
    We will march thro' the valley in peace.
2   We will march thro' the valley in peace, (2x)
    Behold I give myself away, and, ...
3   We will march thro' the valley in peace, (2x)
    This track I'll see and I'll pursue; ...
4   We will march thro' the valley in peace, (2x)
    When I'm dead and buried in the cold silent tomb,
    I don't want you to grieve for me.
                    (Allen, Ware, and Garrison 1867, 73)

Prayer Focus: You did form me in my mother's womb.
I praise you, for I am wonderfully made! Search me, O
God, lead in the way of everlasting.

BIOY: 1 Thessalonians 3–5 (344/21)

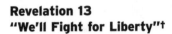

Revelation 13
"We'll Fight for Liberty"†

WE'LL fight for liberty,
We'll fight for liberty,
We'll fight for liberty,
Till the Lord shall call us home;
We'll soon be free,
Till the Lord shall call us home.

(Southern 1997, 214)

† Over the years the slaves had developed a sizable repertory of songs about the day when freedom should come. While few songs texts of this kind are preserved, and understandably so, there are numerous references to them. As the war tensions mounted throughout the nation, black folk were restricted more and more. In Georgetown, South Carolina, for example, slaves were whipped for singing this spiritual on the occasion of Lincoln's election.

Prayer Focus: We who believe in freedom cannot rest: the spirit of the beast and false prophet lives.

BIOY: 2 Thessalonians 1-3 (345/20)

Psalm 140
"Weary Traveler"

LET us cheer the weary traveler,
Cheer the weary traveler:
Let us cheer the weary traveler,
Along the heavenly way.

1 I'll take my gospel trumpet,
   An' I'll begin to blow,
   An' if my Saviour helps me,
   I'll blow wherever I go.

2 An' brothers if you meet with crosses,
   An' trials on the way,
   Just keep your trust in Jesus,
   An' don't forget to pray.

(Johnson and Johnson 1925, 184)

Prayer Focus: Lord, thank you for maintaining the cause of the afflicted and justice for the poor. Surely evil will hunt the violent and overthrow them. I give you thanks for our fellowship. It's a joy divine!

BIOY: 1 Timothy 1-3 (346/19)

Revelation 14
"Were You There When They Crucified My Lord?"

1 WERE you there, when they crucified my Lord?
   Were you there, when they crucified my Lord?
   Oh, Sometimes, it causes me to tremble, tremble.
   Were you there, when they crucified my Lord?
2 Were you there,
        when they nailed him to the tree? ...
3 Were you there,
        when they pierced him in the side? ...
4 Were you there,
        when the sun refused to shine? ...
5 Were you there,
        when they laid him in the tomb? ...

(Johnson and Johnson 1926, 136)

Prayer Focus: Lord, it also causes me to tremble when I think about all that you endured on the cross. I tremble when I think about all those mob lynchings of black people. Mercy!

BIOY: 1 Timothy 4-6 (347/18)

Psalm 141
"What a Trying Time"

1   O ADAM, where are you?
    Adam, where are you?
    Adam, where are you?
    O what a trying time!
2   Lord, I am in the garden, (3x) ...
3   Adam, you ate that apple, (3x) ...
4   Lord, Eve she gave it to me, (3x) ...
5   Adam, it was forbidden, (3x) ...
6   Lord said, walk out de garden, (3x) ...
               (Allen, Ware, and Garrison 1867, 74)

Prayer Focus: When the fullness of time came, O mighty God, you sent forth your Son, born of a virgin woman, to redeem slaves of sin that we might receive the adoption as your children and cry unto you, Abba, Father. We are no longer slaves, but heirs to the riches of your glory through Christ (cf. Gal. 4:4–7). I'm standing on your promises!

BIOY: 2 Timothy 1-4 (348/17)

Revelation 15
"What Yo' Gwine to Do
When Yo' Lamp Burn Down?"
(Matt. 25:1-13)

O, PO' sinner,
O, now is yo' time,
O, po' sinner,
O, What yo' gwine to do
when yo' lamp burn down.

1   Fin' de Eas', fin' de Wes',
    What yo' gwine to do when yo' lamp burn down.
    Fire gwine to burn down de wilderness,
    What yo' gwine to do when yo' lamp burn down.

2   Head got wet wid de midnight dew, ...
    Mornin' star was a witness too, ...

3   Dey whipp'd Him up an
            dey whipp'd Him down, ...
    Dey whipp'd dat man all ovah town, ...

4   Dey nail'd His han' and dey nail'd His feet, ...
    De hammer was heard on Jerusalem street, ...

                    (Johnson and Johnson 1925, 170)

Prayer Focus: How great and marvelous you are!

BIOY: Titus 1-3; Philemon 1 (349/16)

Psalm 142
"When the Lord Shall Appear"

CHILDREN, we all shall be free, (3x)
When the Lord shall appear.

1   We want no cowards in our band,
    That from their colors fly,
    We call for valiant-hearted men,
    That are not afraid to die.

2   We see the pilgrim as he lies,
    With glory in his soul;
    To heav'n he lifts his longing eyes,
    And bids this world adieu.

3   Give ease to the sick, give sight to the blind,
    Enable the cripple to walk;
    He'll raise the dead from under the earth,
    And give them permission to fly.

(Boatner and Townsend 1927, 50)

Prayer Focus: Oh, deep in my heart, I do believe, that some day your face I shall see; from tears I shall be free!

BIOY: Hebrews 1-4 (350/15)

DAY 351

Revelation 16
"When the Saints Go Marching In"

1   O WHEN the saints, go marching in,
      O when the saints go marching in,
      Lord, I want to be in that number,
      When the saints go marching in.
      I have a loving *brother,*
      He has gone on before,
      And I promised I would meet *him.*
      When the saints go marching in.

2   O when they crown, Him Lord of all, ...
      I have a loving *sister, ... She ... her ...*

3   O when the sun, refuse to shine, ...
      I have a loving *father, ... He ... him ...*

4   O when the moon, runs down in blood, ...
      I have a loving *mother, ... She ... her ...*

           (Boatner and Townsend 1927, 33)

Prayer Focus: O Lord, I want to be in that number when you are crowned Lord and King of all!

BIOY: Hebrews 5–8 (351/14)

Psalm 143
"When We Do Meet Again"

WHEN we do meet again,
When we do meet again,
When we do meet again,
'Twill be no more to part.
Brother Billy, fare you well,
Brother Billy, fare you well,
We'll sing hallelujah,
when we do meet again.

(Allen, Ware, and Garrison 1867, 41)

Prayer Focus: Lord, the traumatic breakup of the families and friends, as experienced by victims of the slave trade, is like a deeply inflicted wound piercing even to the division of the soul and spirit. Oh what misery to the soul is the involuntary physical separation of loved ones! Lord, when we all get to heaven, what a day of rejoicing that'll be! By and by when the morning comes, it will be howdy, howdy and never good-bye!

BIOY: Hebrews 9-11 (352/13)

Revelation 17
"Where Shall I Be
When de Firs' Trumpet Soun'?"

1 WHERE shall I be when de firs' trumpet soun'
Where shall I be,
When it soun' so loud,
When it soun' so loud
til it wake up de dead;
Where shall I be when it soun'. (O Bretheren ...)

2 Gwine to try on ma robe
when de firs' trumpet soun'
Gwine to try on ma robe,
When it soun' so loud,
When it soun' so loud
til it wake up de dead;
Where shall I be when it soun'. (O Sisteren ...)

(Johnson and Johnson 1925, 136)

Prayer Focus: I got a new robe over in glory. As soon as the trumpet sounds, I'm going to put on my new robe. I can't wait to try it on!

BIOY: Hebrews 12-13 (353/12)

Psalm 144
"Who Dat a-Comin' Ovah Yondah?"

1. O, WHO dat a-comin' ovah yondah,
   Hallelujah, O, hallelu:
      O, who dat a-comin' ovah yondah,
      O, who dat a-comin' ovah yondah,
      O, who dat a-comin' ovah yondah, Hallelu.
2. O, don't dat a-look-a like my sister,
   Hallelujah, O, hallelu:
      O, don't dat a-look-a like my sister, ...
3. O, don't dat a-look-a like my brother,
   Hallelujah, O, hallelu:
      O, don't dat a-look-a like my brother, ...

(Johnson and Johnson 1925, 104)

Prayer Focus: Lord, when I look over yonder, I pray that I'll see a whole bunch of angels a' coming after me. And if I see some folks all dressed in red, I pray they've been redeemed by the blood once shed.

BIOY: James 1–5 (354/11)

Revelation 18
"Who is on the Lord's Side?"

LET me tell you what is nat'rally de fac'
Who is on de Lord's side,
None o' God's chil'n nebber look back,
Who is on de Lord's side.

1 Way in de walley,
   Who is on de Lord's side,
   Way in de walley,
   Who is on de Lord's side.

2 Weepin' Mary, …

3 Mournin' Marta, …

4 Risen Jesus, …

(Allen, Ware, and Garrison 1867, 56)

Prayer Focus: Mountain get out of my way! Hit the road, Jack, and never come back. I once was lost, on my way to hell, but now I'm found and bound for glory land. Lord, I'll never look back! I'm determined to make heaven my home. Whatever it takes Lord, do it.

BIOY: 1 Peter 1-2 (355/10)

Psalm 145
"Who'll Be a Witness for My Lord?"

MY soul is a witness for my Lord,
MY soul is a witness for my Lord,
MY soul is a witness for my Lord,
MY soul is a witness for my Lord,

1   You read in de Bible an' you understan',
    Methuselah was de oldes' man,
    He lived nine-hundred an' sixty nine,
    He died an' went to heaven, Lord, in-a due time.
    O, Methuselah was a witness for my Lord, (3x)
    O, Methuselah was a witness for my Lord.

2   You read in de Bible an' you understan',
        Samson was de strongest man;
    Samson went out at-a one time, An' he killed
    about a thousan' of de Philistine,
    Delilah fooled Samson, dis we know,
        For de Holy Bible tells us so,
    She shaved off his head jus' as clean as yo' han',
    An' his strength became de same
        as any natch'al man.
    O, Samson was a witness for my Lord, (3x)
    O, Samson was a witness for my Lord.

continued

3   Daniel was a Hebrew child,
        He went to pray to his God awhile,
    De king at once for Daniel did sen',
        An' he put him right down in de lion's den;
    God sent His angels de lions for to keep,
        An' Daniel laid down an' went to sleep.
    Now Daniel was a witness for my Lord, (3x)
    Now Daniel was a witness for my Lord.
    O, who'll be a witness for my Lord? (2x)
    My soul is a witness for my Lord, (2x)
                (Johnson and Johnson 1925, 130)

Prayer Focus: Lord, I'll be a witness for you in everything that I do.

BIOY: 1 Peter 3-5 (356/9)

Revelation 19
"Will the Lighthouse Shine on Me?"

SHINE on me, shine on me,
I wonder if the lighthouse will shine on me!
Oh, shine on me, shine on me,
I wonder if the lighthouse will shine on me!

1   I heard the voice of Jesus say,
        "Come unto Me, and rest;
    Lay down, thou weary on, lay down
    Thy head upon my breast."

2   I came to Jesus as I was,
        Weary, and worn and sad;
    I found in Him a resting place,
    And He has made me glad.

3   I heard the voice of Jesus say,
        "Behold, I freely give,
    The living water, thirsty one,
    Stoop down, and drink, and live!"

4   I came to Jesus and I drank,
        Of that, life-giving stream;
    My thirst was quenched, my soul revived,
    And now I live in Him.

(Boatner and Townsend 1927, 49)

Prayer Focus: Lord, let your light shine on me.

BIOY: 2 Peter 1-3 (357/8)

Psalm 146
"Witness for My Lord"

WITNESS, for my Lord, Witness, for my Lord,
Witness, for my Lord;
O, my soul is a witness for my Lord.

1   O, I haven't been to Heav'n but I've been told,
    My soul is a witness for my Lord;
    That the streets are pearl
    and the gates are gold,
    My soul is a witness for my Lord.

2   I want to go to Heaven and I want to go right, ...
    I want to go to Heav'n all dressed in white, ...

3   There isn't but the one thing
            that grieves my mind, ...
    My mother's gone to Heav'n
            and left me behind, ...

(Boatner and Townsend 1927, 34)

Prayer Focus: Like herald angels my soul doth sing!

BIOY: 1 John 1-5 (358/7)

DAY 359

Revelation 20
"Woke Up Dis Mornin'"

1 OH, I woke up dis mornin' wid mah min',
  (An' it was) stayed on Jesus,
  Woke up this mornin' wid mah min',
   Stayed on Jesus,
  Woke up this mornin' wid mah min',
   Stayed on Jesus,
  Hallelu, Hallelu, Hallelujah.

2 Can't hate your neighbor in your min',
  (if you keep it) stayed on Jesus, ...

3 Makes you love everybody with your min',
  (when you keep it) stayed on Jesus, ...

4 De devil can't catch you in your min',
  (if you keep it) stayed on Jesus, ...

5 Jesus is de captain in your min',
  (when you keep it) stayed on Jesus, ...

      (Songs of Zion 1981, 146)

Prayer Focus: You are worthy of all praise!

BIOY: 2 John; 3 John; Jude (359/6)

361

DAY 360

Psalm 147
"Wrestle on Jacob" (Gen. 32:28)

1 I HOLD my brudder* wid a tremblin' han',
   De Lord will bless my soul.†
   Wrastl' on, Jacob, Jacob, day is a-breakin',
   Wrastl' on, Jacob,
   Oh, he** would not let him go.
2 I will not let you go, my Lord, ...
3 Fisherman Peter out at sea, ...
4 He cast†† all night and he cast†† all day, ...
5 He‡ catch no fish, but he‡ catch some soul, ...
6 Jacob hang from a tremblin' limb, ...

                    (Allen, Ware, and Garrison 1867, 4)

   * My sister, Brudder Jacky, All de member
   † I would not let him go
  ** Lord I
  †† Fish
   ‡ I

Prayer Focus: I won't give up! I won't give in. My hope
is built; I'm standing on the promises.

BIOY: Revelation 1–3 (360/5)

Revelation 21
"You Go, I'll Go wid You"

YOU go, I'll go wid you;
Open yo' mouth, I'll speak for you:
Lord, if I go, tell me what to say,
Dey won't believe in me. (Oh)

1   Now Lord, I give myself to Thee,
    'Tis all dat I can do;
    If thou should draw thyself from me,
    Oh, wither shall I flee?

2   De archangels done droop dere wings,
    Went up on Zion's hill to sing;
    Climbin' Jacob's ladder high,
    Gwine reach heab'n by an' by.

(Johnson and Johnson 1926, 44)

Prayer Focus: Lord, you are the Alpha and Omega, the Beginning and the End. I thirst!

BIOY: Revelation 4-7 (361/4)

Psalm 148
"You Got a Right"

YOU got a right, I got a right,
We all got a right, to the tree of life. (Yes)
De very time I thought I was los',
De dungeon shuck an' de chain fell off.
You may hinder me here
But you cannot dere,
'Cause God in de heav'n
gwinter answer prayer. (O bretheren/O sisteren)
(Johnson and Johnson 1925, 183)

Prayer Focus: Lord, I am somebody! I may not be rich. I may not live in a big house. I may not drive a fancy car, but I am somebody! I have been created in your image and, through Christ, I have rights. I will respect you by respecting myself and demanding that my unalienable rights be protected.

BIOY: Revelation 8-11 (362/3)

Revelation 22
"You Hear the Lambs a-Cryin'"
(John 21:15-17)

*YOU hear the lambs a-cryin',
    hear the lambs a-cryin',
hear the lambs a-cryin', O Shepherd,
    feed my sheep.*

1 My Savior spoke these words so sweet,
   Oo ... O Shepherd, feed my sheep,
   "Peter, if you love me, feed my sheep."
   Oo ... O Shepherd, feed my sheep.

2 Lord, I love Thee, Thou dost know;
   Oo ... O Shepherd, feed my sheep,
   O give me grace to love Thee more,
   Oo ... O Shepherd, feed my sheep.

3 Wasn't that an awful shame?
   Oo ... O Shepherd, feed my sheep,
   He hung three hours in mortal pain.
   Oo ... O Shepherd, feed my sheep.

(Songs of Zion 1981, 128)

Prayer Focus: Feed me that I may feed another.

BIOY: Revelation 12-14 (363/2)

Psalm 149
"You May Bury Me in de Eas'"

1   YOU may bury me in de Eas',
    You may bury in de Wes',
    But I'll hear de trumpet soun' in dat mornin',
    In dat mornin', my Lord,
    How I long to go,
    For to hear de trumpet soun',
    In dat mornin'.
2   Good ole Christians in dat day,
    Dey'll take wings an' fly away,
    For to hear de trumpet soun', ...
                            (Johnson and Johnson 1925, 181)

Prayer Focus: My Lord, my God, oh, how I long to hear that trumpet sound, and have my soul leave this dust of the ground. Oh, how I long for that happy day when all my tears you will wipe away! What a great getting up morning that will be. Hallelujah!

BIOY: Revelation 15-18 (364/1)

Psalm 150
"You Mus' Hab Dat True Religion"

YOU mus' hab' dat true religion,
You mus' hab' yo' soul converted,
You mus' hab dat true religion,
You can't cross dere. (O, yes, you)

1 Whar you gwine po' sinnah,
 Whar you gwine, I say,
 I'm a gwine down to de ribbuh ob Jord'n,
 You can't cross dere.

2 Whar you gwine po' liar, …

3 Whar you gwine po' gambler, …

4 Whar you gwine back slider, …

(Johnson and Johnson 1926, 100)

Prayer Focus: I thank you, Jesus. Thank you, Lord! You brought me from a mighty long way! Thank you, Sir Jesus, for giving me grace to finish this race. I can take the pain and the heartache. I've got to run on now. I'll see you up yonder—soon!

BIOY: Revelation 19-22 (365/0)

"'Zekiel Saw de Wheel"

1 WHEEL, oh, wheel,
   Wheel in de middle of a wheel;
   Wheel, oh, wheel,
   Wheel in de middle of a wheel.
2 'Zekiel saw de wheel of time, …
   Ev'ry spoke was humankind, ….
3 'Way up yonder on de mountain top, …
   My Lord spoke an' de chariot stop, …
   'Zekiel saw de wheel,
       'Way up in de middle of de air,
   'Zekiel saw de wheel,
       'Way up in de middle of de air.
   De big wheel run by faith,
       Little wheel run by de grace of God;
   Wheel widin a wheel,
       'Way in de middle of de air.
                         (Johnson and Johnson 1926, 144)

Negro Hymn of Judgment Day

1   DONE yo' see de chariot ridin' on de clouds?
     De wheels in de fire how dey roll, how dey roll!
     O dat mornin' you'll hyar a mighty roarin',
     Dat'll be de earth a-burnin',
     When de Heabens fly away.

2   Done yo' hyar de trumpets blowin' fo' de dade?
     Done yo' hyar de bones how dey shake,
          how dey shake!
     O dat mornin' you'll hyar a mighty roarin', ...

3   Done yo' see de graves dey open
          an' de dade arisin'?
     An' de bones in de fyar how dey burn,
          how dey burn!
     O dat mornin' you'll hyar a mighty roarin', ...

4   Done yo' see de eyes throo de lids how dey stare?
     An' de living worms how dey gnaws,
          how dey gnaws!
     O dat mornin' you'll hyar a mighty roarin', ...

5   Done yo' see de king a-comin' on de clouds?
     See de nail prints in his han's how dey shine,
          how dey shine!
     O dat mornin' you'll hyar a mighty roarin', ...

6   Done yo' see his robes a-flowin' on de light?
     An' he hade an' he hair white as snow,
          white as snow!
     O dat mornin' you'll hyar a mighty roarin', ...

(Lovell 1972, 380)

Hymn of Dedication

"There is Hope"

1   EVERYONE, have their ups and downs,
All of life's ups, outweigh the downs,
But when trouble's around, I do believe,
Seem like the ups, don't outweigh the downs.

2   At times when life is hard,
And friends can't be found,
Look all around, find you're alone,
I have good news, I do believe,
If you pray (to God), Down on bended knee.

3   "Hear me Lord, hear me pray,
I need You today,
Comfort and give me strength to carry on,
I confess my sins, And invite You in,
Now this fight, Is yours to win."

4   "I was blind, now I see,
With You I have victory,
Life is worth the living, even when it rains,
I do proclaim, Without any shame,
Jesus is my Lord, And He is my King!"

5   Don't you see, just like me,
That life is one big symphony,
Jesus is Lord of lords and King of kings,
Yes I have good news,
For everyone, There is hope,
In the name of God's Son.

© 2000 Leonidas A. Johnson

Hymns of Benediction

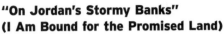

"On Jordan's Stormy Banks"
(I Am Bound for the Promised Land)
(In Old Meter Call-and-Response Fashion)

1   ON Jordan's stormy banks I stand.
And cast a wishful eye,
To Canaan's fair and happy land,
Where my possessions lie.

2   All o'er those wide extended plains,
Shines one eternal day;
There God the Son forever reigns,
And scatters night away.

3   No chilling winds, nor pois'nous breath,
Can reach that healthful shore;
Sickness and sorrow, pain and death,
Are felt and feared no more.

4   When shall I reach that happy place,
And be forever blest?
When shall I see my Father's face,
And in His bosom rest?

5   Filled with delight, my raptured soul,
Would here no longer stay;
Tho' Jordan's waves around me roll,
Fearless I'd launch away.

"We Shall Overcome"

In Unison

1 WE shall overcome, we shall overcome,
   we shall overcome someday!
   Oh, deep in my heart I do believe
   we shall overcome someday!
2 We'll walk hand in hand, ...
3 We shall all be free, ...
4 We shall live in peace, ...
5 The Lord will see us through, ...

(The AME Zion Bicentennial Hymnal 1996, 640)

"The Lord watch between me and thee when we are absent one from another." Amen.

—Genesis 31:49

I free, I free!
I free as a frog
I free till I fool
Glory Alleluia!

(Lovell 1972, 116)

"... you *are* a chosen generation, a royal priesthood. a holy nation, His own special people, that you may proclaim the praises of Him who called you out of darkness into His marvelous light; who once *were* not a people but now *are* the people of God, who had not obtained mercy but now have obtained mercy."

—1 Peter 2:9–10

"I *am* the L ORD your God, who brought you out of the land of Egypt, that *you* should not be their slaves; I have boken the bands of your yoke and made you walk upright."

—Leviticus 26:13

Bibliography

The African Methodist Episcopal Zion Bicentennial Hymnal. By The Rt. Rev. George W. Walker, Sr, Chairman, Bicentennial Hymnal Commission. The African Methodist Episcopal Zion Church, 1996.

Allen, James, Hilton Als, John Lewis and Leon F. Litwack. *Without Sanctuary: Lynching Photography in America.* New Mexico: Twin Palms Publishers, 2000.

Allen, William Francis, Charles Pickard Ware, and Lucy McKim Garrison, eds., *Slave Songs of the United States.* 1867; reprint Bedford: Applewood Books, 1996.

Berlin, Ira, Marc Favreau, and Steven F. Miller, eds. *Remembering Slavery: African Americans Talk About Their Personal Experiences of Slavery and Freedom* (A Book and Audiotape Set). New York: The New Press in conjunction with the Library of Congress and as a companion to Smithsonian Productions's radio documentary, 1998.

Boatner, Edward and Willa A. Townsend, eds. *Spirituals Triumphant Old and New.* Nashville: National Baptist Convention, USA, Sunday School Publishing Board, 1921.

Johnson, James Weldon and J. Rosamond Johnson. *The Book of American Negro Spirituals.* New York: The Viking Press, 1925; unabridged republication, New York: DaCapo Press, Inc., 1969.

Johnson, James Weldon and J. Rosamond Johnson. *The Second Book of Negro Spirituals*. New York: The Viking Press, 1926; unabridged republication, New York: DaCapo Press, Inc., 1969.

Lovell, John. *Black Song: The Forge and the Flame*. New York: The MacMillan Co., 1972.

National Baptist Convention, USA, Sunday School Publishing Board. *Gospel Pearls*. Nashville: Sunday School Publishing Board, 1921.

The New National Baptist Hymnal. Nashville: The National Baptist Publishing Board, 1977.

Songs of Zion. William B. McClain, Chairman, The National Advisory Task Force on the Hymnbook Project. Nashville: Abingdon Press, 1982.

Southern, Eileen. *The Music of Black Americans: A History*. 2d ed. New York: W.W. Norton & Company, 1983.

Warren, Gwendolin Sims. *Ev'ry Time I Feel the Spirit: 101 Best-Loved Psalms, Gospel Hymns, and Spiritual Songs of the African American Church*. New York: Henry Holt and Company, Inc., 1997.

Wyatt, Walker Tee. *Somebody's Calling My Name: Black Sacred Music and Social Change*. Valley Forge: Judson Press, 1979.

Reference Sound Recordings

Mt. Tabor Missionary Baptist Church, Los Angeles, California. Rev. Dr. E. E. Stafford, Pastor. *A Glorious Journey* [CD]. Inglewood, California: Cold Wave Record Enterprise, 1998.

Reagon, Bernice Johnson ed., (1989 and 1992) *Wade in the Water: Volume I, African American Spirituals: The Concert Tradition; Volume II, African American Congregational Singing: Nineteenth-Century Roots; Volume III, African American Gospel: The Pioneering Composers; Volume IV, Community Gospel* [four-CD set]. Washington: Smithsonian Folkways Recordings, in collaboration with National Public Radio, Center for Folklife Programs and Cultural Studies.

Index

387

Addendum

Hymn of Dedication

Hymns of Benediction